Dennis's
TO LOWER YOUR
FAT THERMOSTAT

Desserts
TO LOWER YOUR
FAT THERMOSTAT

Written By
Barbara W. Higa, R.D.

Introduction By
Dennis W. Remington, M.D.

Copyright 1988 by
Vitality House International, Inc.
1675 N. Freedom Blvd. #11-C
Provo, Utah 84604

Telephone: 801-373-5100
To Order: Call Toll Free 1-800-637-0708

First Printing, September, 1988

Second Printing, June, 1989

This cookbook is a collection of recipes which have been gathered from various sources. Recipes have been adapted to meet a no-sugar, low-fat, high complex carbohydrate, low-sodium criteria.

Library of Congress Catalog Card Number:

ISBN 0-912547-06-5

Printed in the United States of America

Front Cover: Apricot-Date Cookies, p. 6; Fruit Tart, p. 32; Pumpkin Oatmeal Bread, p. 184; Fruit Bars, p. 13; Pineapple "Sherbet", p. 91; Sparkling Punch, p. 125.

Table of Contents

About the Author

Barbara W. Higa, Registered Dietitian, works in a medical practice with patients suffering from food and chemical allergies, obesity, and yeast problems. A graduate of Brigham Young University, she completed her dietetic internship at the Veterans Administration Hospital in Los Angeles, and taught quantity food production at Brigham Young University. She has instructed physicians from the United States, Canada, and Australia on new allergy treatment and yeast treatment techniques. She lectures on sound nutrition and exercise principles. She specializes in developing delicious recipes for healthy eating. She is the mother of four children. She is a coauthor of *Back to Health - A Comprehensive Medical and Nutritional Yeast Control Program* and *The Bitter Truth About Artificial Sweeteners.*

Foreword

For six years I have worked closely with several thousand people suffering from food and chemical allergies, obesity, and yeast overgrowth. As we help these patients strengthen their immune system, three of our primary concerns are diet, exercise, and stress control.

Generally one of the first lifestyle changes we ask these patients to make is to completely eliminate sugar and artificial sweeteners. Why? One reason is that people begin to enjoy the good taste of healthy foods if they are not eating foods that are very sweet. Fruits, vegetables and grains don't taste very good when you are eating a large amount of sugar. But when you eliminate high levels of sweet, food suddenly begins to taste better!

Dennis Remington, M.D. and I also wrote a book entitled, *The Bitter Truth About Artificial Sweeteners*. In its aftermath, we have spoken with hundreds of people nationwide who have had health problems associated with the use of artificial sweeteners. As we went on the publicity tour associated with that book, we constantly were asked, "I'm a diabetic. If artificial sweeteners aren't good for me, what can I do?" Weight control patients who found they were addicted to sugar or cola-caffeine asked the same question: "Will I ever get to eat sweet products again?" That's how this book evolved: I wanted to provide a way to have something sweet <u>without</u> using sugar, honey, fructose, or artificial sweeteners.

This project was not without dilemma. Could I provide something sweet without compromising a patients health? Other books on the market gave ideas on how to do this, but patients commonly complain that the recipes taste terrible and are anything but sweet. That's not all: some recipes eliminated the sugar but used refined flour and were high in fat content. We have found no other book on the market that features desserts and other treats that are low in fat, high in complex carbohydrates, and that contain neither salt nor artificial sweeteners.

All recipes were formulated at 4,500 feet above sea level. Those of you who are living in high altitudes shouldn't have to make any adjustments in the recipes. Those living at sea level should not have any problems either.

Some clarification needs to be made so that you can understand the recipes very clearly. A fruit juice is one that is ready to drink and already diluted. Check your local grocery store and health food store. A variety of available brands have no added sugar.

A fruit concentrate is found in frozen form in your grocery store's freezer section. If the recipe calls for a fruit concentrate, use it without diluting it. Thaw it out, measure it, and use as is. You can use a portion of a can; simply cover what's left and put it back in the freezer. A 12-oz can provides 1 1/2 cups of concentrate.

Whole wheat flour may be purchased in a regular grocery store in the flour section. If you have access to a grinder, you can grind your own if you so desire. Other whole grains may be found in health food stores. If you have not previously used whole grains for yourself or your family, you will want to start out by making the recipes with half whole wheat flour and half unbleached white flour. This will allow time for your gastrointestinal tracts to become accustomed to the increase in fiber. As you begin to enjoy this combination of flours, then make the recipe with all whole grains.

Please Note: **The amount of whole wheat flour that you will use may vary in these recipes.** Sometimes you might have a very low moisture whole wheat flour and you will use less than called for in the recipe. If you were to use a different brand of whole wheat flour, it may be just right. As you gain experience in using whole grains, you will recognize what amount to use. If the batter starts to look thick, don't use as much flour; if it looks too thin, then add a little more.

Nuts are a source of protein and are high in healthy natural oils. They come in a variety of tastes and textures. I always recommend getting unprocessed nuts; if you want them roasted, roast them in your oven. To roast nuts, spread them on a baking sheet and bake at 350° for 5 to 10 minutes. Always watch them carefully, or the nuts may burn. Processed nuts are often deep-fat fried and add very unhealthy oils to a good food product. Because nuts are naturally high in oil, most of the recipes have nuts as an optional ingredient. You can decide whether to add nuts to any of the recipes. It stands to reason that a gram of a good healthy oil is not going to be used by the body in the same manner as a gram of a saturated fat, but when it comes to recipe calculations, they look exactly the same. With the increased research on the fats and oils, there may someday be a distinction between types of oils--but, for now, there is none.

Cold-pressed oils are polyunsaturated fats which have not gone through the hydrogenation process. They contain essential fatty acids that promote the formation of healthy prostaglandins, types of hormones necessary to the immune system. Prostaglandins are critical for health because they are involved with reproduction, fertility, inflammation, immunity, and intracellular communication. Any of these processes can break down without enough essential fatty acids. Commercial oils, margarine, and vegetable shortenings found on the grocery store shelves are hydrogenated. Some varieties of cold-pressed oils include safflower, soybean, linseed, walnut, and sunflower. The label will list the oil as cold-pressed if it falls into this category. A cold-pressed oil must be refrigerated after it is opened. Olive oil is also very healthy and can be used in any of the recipes calling for cold-pressed oil. Cold-pressed oils may be purchased in health food stores and many supermarket's health food section carries these products.

I have included two sets of calculations. The first set is based on the scoring system featured in *How to Lower Your Fat Thermostat*. **RCU** stands for Refined Carbohydrate Units. 1 RCU = 6 grams of sugar or honey; OR 12 grams of white flour; OR 24 grams of raisins or dates. According to Fat Thermostat guidelines you are allowed 2 RCU's per day. **FU** stands for Fat Unit. 1 FU = 6 grams of refined fat such as oil or margarine; OR 8 grams of naturally occurring fat such as meat, milk, or eggs. You are allowed 4 FUs per day if you weigh less than 140 pounds and 5 FUs per day if you weigh more than 140 pounds. For further information, you will want to refer to the Table of Food Composition p. 187 - 208 in *How to Lower Your Fat Thermostat*.

Cal represents the number of calories in each serving, and **% Fat** represents the percentage of the total calories in that recipe derived from fat sources. **P, F,** and **C** represent the grams of protein, fat, and carbohydrate respectively for each serving of the recipe. **Na** represents the number of milligrams of sodium in each serving. **T** indicates that there is only a trace (less than 1 gram) of a nutrient.

The second set of calculations is based on the Diabetic Exchange System. If you are a diabetic, consult your physician to see if you can simply fit the exchanges into your daily meal pattern. These recipes provide a way for you to have something sweet to enjoy that you can still metabolize safely. These recipes are also great alternatives for people with hypoglycemia.

The recipes have no added sodium, which is conducive with guidelines given by the American Heart Association. Salt is a major contributor to the problem of high blood pressure (hypertension).

The recipes in this book provide you with naturally occurring sweet alternatives. They are in no way to be substituted for good healthy foods such as meats, fish, poultry, vegetables, grains, milk products, legumes, and so on. They are to be used in conjunction with wise food choices as an occasional sweet and healthy snack, treat, or dessert. If you are under medical care, consult your physician before making any dietary changes.

With every man, woman, and child in this country eating an average of 125 pounds of sugar every year, this book offers possibilities for better nutrition and improved health for all of us.

Acknowledgements

Many thanks to Kathy Frandsen for her editing skills and for the speed with which she edits.

To Mitch Stowell for superior abilities in giving advice and direction to book layouts. Only a great friend would sacrifice time with his family to assist in accomplishing deadline goals.

To Margaret Wagner and Dana Wong for helping to prepare recipes and for love and support beyond the call-of-duty.

To Dorothy Sudweeks, Jolayne Remington, Karen Murdock, Sylvia Cundick, and Velora Smith for their ideas and constant encouragement.

To Rick Thayne for his cover design graphics.

To Borge Andersen Photography Studios for producing exceptional photographs.

To food stylist Janet Schaap for her ability to construct settings that make each picture unique and exciting.

To K.J. Smith, who kept everything running.

To John Webb and The Training, who taught me to explore all possibilities, break through all the barriers, and "go-for-it."

A special thanks to Dennis Remington, friend and colleague, who took a risk and encouraged the possibilities in me.

Introduction

Between the covers of this book are two hundred delicious recipes for desserts, treats, snacks, drinks, and goodies. None of them contain refined sugar, artificial sweeteners, or salt, and they are low in fat.

One of Barbara's hobbies is to duplicate the taste of delicious desserts while substituting healthy ingredients for the high fats and high sugars they usually contain. Over the last five years that we have worked together in a nutrition-oriented medical practice, I have had the opportunity of tasting many of these recipes. They are not only healthy and taste good, but, in my opinion, taste better than most of the traditional recipes that they replace.

These recipes all fit within the guidelines suggested by various health agencies, including the American Heart Association, the American Cancer Society, and the American Diabetes Association. These organizations have all recommended that we cut down our consumption of fats, refined sugar, and salt, and that we increase our consumption of fiber and complex carbohydrates (contained in vegetables, whole grains, legumes, and fruit).

I am convinced that many people are needlessly depriving themselves of the pleasures associated with eating in their attempts to lose weight and be healthy. In many cases, they are making themselves fatter and sick with their misdirected efforts. What follows is new information about important factors which everyone should know about taste, satisfaction, and nutrition as they relate in preventing serious physical and emotional health problems. You'll also find important guidelines that will help you use this book to the best advantage.

Refined Sugars - There are various types of sugars manufactured and stored in plants which are useful for human nutrition. In addition to the sugars which they contain, grains, vegetables, and fruits also contain fiber and a wide range of minerals, vitamins, and other nutrients. Our bodies use mostly sugar in the form of glucose for energy needs. Other sugars and carbohydrate sources, protein, and even some fats can be converted to glucose within our bodies.

The term **sugar** is often used to mean table sugar or sucrose. Sucrose is usually refined from sugar cane or sugar beets. Other refined sugars such as corn syrup or other corn-derived sweeteners, contain high levels of fructose. All of these refined sugars are sweet tasting, but have virtually no remaining fiber, minerals, vitamins, or other healthy nutrients. In some cases, they have unhealthy residues remaining from the manufacturing process. Honey is a refined sugar which is manufactured by bees rather than by humans, but has many of the same problems as other refined sugars. It has a few nutrients, but not a significant amount. It is somewhat sweeter than sucrose, so less can be used in a recipe to give equivalent sweetness levels. Some people who tolerate sucrose very poorly can tolerate honey.

In my medical career, I have worked with more than 7,000 patients who were encouraged to completely stop using refined sugar in their diets. Two things have impressed me. First, it is amazing how many people have a difficult time stopping sugar use, and in many cases, all the features of addiction are present. Second, it is incredible how much better many people feel once they have stopped using refined sugar. A wide range of symptoms have completely disappeared only to immediately return if sugar is used again. Most of these people had no idea that sugar was causing problems for them, because they had used it daily. It wasn't until they stopped it completely for a long enough time to get over the withdrawal effects before they noticed the improvements. All of the recipes in this book are completely free of refined sugars, with the exception of two containing a small amount of honey.

Refined Carbohydrates - There are other refined carbohydrates in addition to refined sugars. White wheat flour, for example, is also highly refined. The outer layer of the wheat kernel is removed along with the wheat germ. These two components of wheat contain a good share of the nutrients important for good health. Whole wheat flour has seven or eight times as much fiber, twice as much calcium, and four times as much magnesium, potassium, and phosphorus as does white flour. Although the iron and some of the vitamins removed during refining are replaced if flour is enriched, no attempt is made to replace all of the nutrients that are removed. The recipes in this book use mostly unrefined carbohydrates, although a few of them contain some refined flour.

Artificial Sweeteners - Over the last few years, especially since the approval of aspartame (NutraSweet), the use of artificial sweeteners has been greatly increased. Hundreds of products are now available with these sweeteners. I have a number of concerns about artificial sweetener use, including the following:

1. Artificial sweeteners seem to contribute to long-term weight gain.[1]

2. They enhance the desire for sweet-tasting foods,[2] and seem to interfere with the enjoyment of less-sweet nutritious food.

3. If diet drinks (or other very low-calorie products) are used as a substitute for eating, it can impair one's nutritional status. I see many patients who use huge amounts of diet pop each day in this way, who eventually develop health problems which I believe are due to malnourishment.

4. I do not believe that the safety of artificial sweeteners has been adequately proven. Saccharine has been shown to cause cancer in some experimental animals,[3,4] and only strong protest from certain individuals prevented it from being removed from the market. FDA approval of aspartame in 1981 came about in spite of the concerns of a number of scientists about potential dangers.

Although the manufacturers of aspartame advertise it as being "made from nature," it is actually composed of two amino acids which are never found in nature by themselves. These molecules, both of which are highly toxic to the human brain, are chemically combined in a laboratory. When a molecule of aspartame is metabolized, a molecule of highly toxic methyl alcohol (wood alcohol) is released. Those people promoting aspartame claim that it would take at least the amount contained in 700 cans of diet pop before any dangers could result. To the contrary, I believe that many people can be adversely affected by this product, especially because of its potential to disrupt the balance of amino acids in the brain, and thus the balance of brain chemicals (neurotransmitters) which are made from amino acids.

5. A great number of people suffer potentially dangerous side effects from using artificial sweeteners. In many cases, these side effects begin many months after starting to use them, and may come on so gradually that the link to the sweeteners is not recognized for a long period of time.

Although most sugar-free recipes for dessert items contain artificial sweeteners, **none** of the recipes in this book contain them. If you decide to use any artificial sweeteners, we encourage you to use very little, and to avoid making products taste very sweet. We believe it is a disservice to give children or diabetics (or any one else, for that matter) highly sweetened foods. It is very difficult to teach children to enjoy vegetables and whole-grain products if they have access to highly sweetened foods. It is hard for everyone to enjoy the wholesome foods which they should be eating if they continue to eat highly sweetened products.

I feel so strongly about artificial sweeteners that Barbara and I spent many months researching and writing a book entitled *The Bitter Truth About Artificial Sweeteners*.[5] The claims we make are detailed and well supported with a great number of references.

Salt - Sodium chloride (NaCl), commonly called salt, is essential to maintain life. Animals which eat strictly plant material have to find extra salt to supplement their plant diet. But humans in the western world typically eat three or more times as much salt as needed. This amount of salt appears to cause a great number of health problems.

One way of evaluating the effect of a product like salt is to compare large population groups who use very little salt with those using a great deal of it. More than twenty populations with very low incidences of blood pressure have been described, all of them eating a low salt diet.[6] In fact, in those populations eating a very low salt diet, there was virtually no elevated blood pressure and no increase in blood pressure with age.[7]

It has been said by some experts that only some people with high blood pressure are salt sensitive. I personally believe that almost everyone with high blood pressure is affected by salt usage, although I do agree that not everyone demonstrates **short-term** blood pressure effects with changes in salt usage.

One patient with high blood pressure continued to have problems in spite of moderate salt restriction, and was started on medication. After a number of months, the unpleasant side effects of the medication prompted him to make dietary changes again. This time, a very strict salt avoidance was successful in lowering his pressure to well within the normal range. It is not just the lowering of salt, however, that produces the blood pressure changes. The ratio between sodium and potassium appears to be very important. Eating foods high in potassium, and preparing those foods in such a way that the potassium is preserved, is also important to dietary control of high blood pressure.

Each cell in our body has to pump sodium out and pump potassium in through the cell membrane in order to survive and function well. Long-term imbalances in sodium and potassium may contribute to a number of other problems besides hypertension, including diabetes, obesity, and heart disease.

The recipes in this book are all very low in sodium, since salt is added as an ingredient in only one recipe. They are thus well suited for anyone on a low-sodium diet.

Many patients have told us that when they got used to using less salt, food tasted better than ever. Salt appears to mask some of the subtleties of foods which make them so delicious and interesting.

Fat - Average Americans eat more than 40 percent of their calories in the form of fat. Most experts agree that this is too much, and are encouraging us to lower our fat intake. Animal fats are high in cholesterol and appear to contribute more to heart disease than do fats from vegetable sources.[8] Fats from plant sources may be a contributor to some types of cancer.[9]

Fat is not all bad, and some fats are essential to maintain life. Some types of fat may actually protect us from heart disease.[10] Fats are used in many parts of our bodies, and various hormones and prostaglandins are produced from fats.

When you eat plant materials which naturally contain fat, you also ingest fiber, carbohydrates, vitamins, minerals, and other important nutrients. When fats are refined from plant sources and used as food, they contain absolutely no vitamins or other important nutrients.

A great deal of exciting information is now coming out on the role of fats in health, which fats are the healthiest, and how these fats are utilized by your body.

Humans have a built-in attraction for high-fat foods. Many desserts and treats are high in fat content. The recipes included in this book are all relatively low in fat content. The fat content of each recipe is listed for those who are interested. Barbara made every effort to use the fats and oils which are the healthiest types known.

THE ROLE OF SWEET TASTE

Humans have an inborn attraction for sweet-tasting food. Some experts believe that this is nature's way of encouraging us to eat foods that are safe, high in nutrients, and high in energy. Most animals (including humans) also have the ability to choose from the foods available the specific ones which will meet their nutritional requirements. Human studies have shown that young children given their choice of various foods will choose a reasonably balanced diet.[11] If refined carbohydrates, sugar, or artificial sweeteners are included, however, children will go for the highly sweet tasting foods to the exclusion of those foods necessary to maintain good health.[12] Experimental rats given only one hour daily to eat will be able to thrive, but if given a choice of food containing sugar, will eat so much of the sugar that they will literally die of malnourishment.[13]

In our society, in which so much refined and highly sweetened foods are available, it is hard for us, and especially our children, to make healthy food choices. To do so, we have to override our basic drives for sweet foods and consciously choose those foods known to be more appropriate. Most children are not mature enough to override their basic drives, and will not eat nutritiously if given free access to highly sweetened foods.

Besides the fact that highly sweet foods are lacking in nutrients, there are a number of other effects of sweet taste within our bodies and brains that you should know about. One very important effect of sweet taste is on the production of insulin. When sweet-tasting substances are ingested, the sweet taste stimulates the pancreas to pour insulin into the bloodstream in anticipation of sugars that will need to be metabolized.[14] This early insulin production has been called the "cephalic phase of insulin release" (cephalic referring to brain). Among other functions, this early insulin release primes the liver so that much of the sugar from the ingested food will be stored in the liver as glycogen.[15] Once all of the sugars have been digested from your intestines, then the fuel needs of your body can be supplied for a number of hours from this glycogen stored in the liver.

If the normal cephalic phase of insulin is interfered with, then several important problems will occur. If there is no cephalic phase of insulin release, very little of the sugar goes into the liver for storage, and there is a rapid rise of sugar in the bloodstream.[16] This triggers an overproduction of insulin. Although insulin is necessary to transport sugar into the cells, insulin excess plays a major role in causing excessive fat storage, and thus weight gain. In an experiment in which two groups of animals were given exactly the same number of calories, those given excess insulin became much fatter.[17] If given free access to food, the food intake and weight gain are even more dramatic in animals given extra insulin.[18]

Although impairment of the cephalic phase of insulin release may cause weight gain, some experts also believe that overstimulation of the cephalic phase of insulin release may also produce obesity.[19] Excessive early insulin production seems to also stimulate fat storage, which could explain how you can make experimental animals fat by giving them sugar or artificially sweetened food.[20] This happens even though no extra calories are given.

One study attempted to identify the reason for the weight gain with refined sugar. Sucrose (table sugar) and polycose (a refined sugar which is not very sweet-tasting) were given to experimental animals. Although both groups got fat, the sweeter-tasting sugar caused more weight gain. When artificial sweeteners were added to the polycose, the animals became considerably fatter than those who ingested the plain polycose.[21] Sweet taste, then, clearly plays a role in weight gain, and it appears that part of the problem is mediated through the cephalic phase of insulin release.

Besides a probable role in overstimulating the cephalic phase of insulin release, refined sugar and artificial sweeteners may interfere in other ways. If you regularly ingest highly sweetened foods, natural foods such as fruit, vegetables, and whole-grain cereals may not taste sweet enough to trigger adequate early release of insulin for normal metabolism.[22] In addition to weight gain, this impairment in sugar metabolism may cause other important problems.

When the glycogen storage in the liver is impaired, and the blood sugar rapidly rises after food ingestion, the resulting overproduction of insulin causes the blood sugar to fall very rapidly. In some cases, this may lead to hypoglycemia (low blood sugar), which can cause very unpleasant symptoms. When there is not enough glucose to provide for the fuel needs of the brain and body, you feel weak, tired, sleepy, have trouble thinking clearly, can't concentrate, and may have speech and coordination impairment. When your blood sugar falls quickly or gets too low, then a number of other hormones are released to break down protein tissue into sugar to keep the blood sugar levels more normal. Overproduction of these hormones (including adrenalin and norepinephrine) may cause symptoms such as fears, panic attacks, nervousness, irritability, sleep disturbance, pounding heart or palpitations, shakiness, and sweating. Rapid changes from high blood sugar to low blood sugar may cause problems like headaches, mood swings, depression, and chronic fatigue.

A very common eating pattern also interferes with normal sugar metabolism. If you go long periods of time between eating, then your sugar stores become depleted, and your body needs to break down protein and fat for your energy needs. As soon as you eat again, the sugar from the ingested food is quickly diverted into the bloodstream in an apparent attempt to replace the depleted stores of muscle and fat. This causes a rapid rise in blood sugar followed by overproduction of insulin. Only after you have replaced these depleted tissues will you then start to store glycogen in normal amounts. This mechanism is a great defense against starvation, and may explain why experimental rats fed only once daily will become much fatter than those given exactly the same number of calories eaten in a number of meals throughout the day.[23]

The tendency to use diet drinks in place of breakfast or lunch may aggravate this tendency for weight gain and impaired sugar metabolism. Even worse may be the direct effect of diet drinks on the cephalic phase of insulin release. This insulin release appears to be, at least in part, a conditioned response.[24] Most people know about conditioned responses because they have heard about Pavlov's experiment with dogs. When he brought them food, he rang a bell at the same time. Soon the dogs became conditioned to the bell ringing and would produce salivation in anticipation of food.

If you use artificial sweeteners in products like diet drinks in which there are very few carbohydrates, at first your body will respond by producing insulin, resulting in a fall in your blood sugar, since there is no sugar absorbed from the diet drink you have just consumed. Your body compensates for the falling blood sugar levels, but after a time, the normal cephalic phase of insulin release appears to be extinguished.[25] This is similar to what Pavlov experienced when he continued to ring the bell but no longer brought food to the dogs. When the bell-ringing was no longer associated with food, the salivation stopped. In a similar way, your response to normal food can thus be greatly impaired by the continued use of artificial sweeteners, leading to weight gain, impaired energy (glycogen) storage, and wildly swinging blood sugar levels.

THE EFFECT OF SWEET TASTE ON BRAIN CHEMISTRY

The balance of certain chemicals or hormones in your brain has a profound effect on your mood and emotions. These same neurohormones also regulate your hunger, eating, and desire for specific foods. When you have a biological need for food, the balance of your brain hormones will change in such a way as to give you a strong desire to eat. This feeling is often associated with restlessness and irritability. When you eat, you will naturally eat until you are totally satisfied (satiated). At this time, you also experience a sense of calmness, relaxation, contentment, happiness, and a sense of well-being which you can get in no other way. If you don't allow yourself to eat until satisfied, you do not obtain these wonderful feelings which appear to be a very important part of good emotional health. This may be an important factor for the irritability, sleep disturbance, preoccupation with food, and the depression suffered by most overweight people who frequently diet.[26]

Sweet taste may also play a role in the hormone changes producing satiety. Someone who is used to eating desserts containing sugar or artificial sweeteners will often find that even a large meal will not be satisfying unless accompanied by some food item which is very sweet. Natural, healthy foods are simply not sweet enough to produce satiety for these habitual sweet eaters.

Hundreds of our patients have described the lack of fulfillment associated with stopping sugars, and the difficult time they have avoiding sweets. Within a week or two, however, very dramatic changes take place if you just faithfully avoid the highly sweetened foods. Healthy foods will begin to taste sweet enough to trigger satiety, so that they will be completely satisfying. Not only that, but these healthy foods will begin to taste delicious, and become much more enjoyable than you would have ever previously imagined possible. Soon, when you are hungry, you will desire good wholesome foods to satisfy that hunger, and won't usually think that much about sweets.

I should point out, however, that most of us retain our natural attraction to high-sweet and high-fat foods. We remember pleasant experiences associated with eating them. If we see them or smell them, we want them. If they are not around, however, we usually won't think much about them if we are regularly satiating ourselves with good, wholesome food.

For many people, the attraction for sweets is so strong that it is like an addiction. In fact, for many people, sugar use has all the characteristic features of addiction. When no sugar has been ingested for a number of hours, there is a strong craving for more sugars. Withdrawal symptoms soon begin, which may include headache, fatigue, weakness, irritability, depression, and even body aches and pains. Ingesting something with sugar can completely eliminate these symptoms within a matter of seconds or minutes. The unpleasant symptoms are replaced by an immense sense of relief, contentment, and relaxation, just like the experience of a drug addict or alcoholic getting a "fix."

The addiction to sugar can be very powerful. One alcoholic patient indicated that it was much harder for her to stop using sugar than it had been for her to stop drinking alcohol. When she finally did get off sugars, she easily lost some weight and began to feel much better than she had felt for years. Hundreds of the patients that we have worked with have also reported feeling much better when they have finally broken the bondage of addiction, whether it is to sugar, sweets in general, caffeine, chocolate, tobacco, alcohol, or drugs. Addiction leads to chronic fatigue, wide swings in energy and emotion, depression, irritability, headaches, and a wide range of other unpleasant symptoms. In addition, addiction results in the guilt and low self esteem associated with dependency and the need to repeatedly find a fix to take away the pain and unpleasantness associated with withdrawal.

I have been amazed at how common sugar and food addictions really are. In talking with our patients and people at seminars and lectures, it is my impression (and that of my staff) that more than 80 percent of the overweight people with whom we work are addicted. In fact, the addiction seems to play a major role in causing the weight gain in the first place, and interfers with effective weight loss. Breaking the addictive cycle is often a major step in beginning effective, long-term weight control.

It is beyond the scope of this introduction to include detailed information about breaking addictive patterns, but good information about this is contained in our book, *The Bitter Truth About Artificial Sweeteners*. We are working experimentally on an exciting new approach to addiction management which holds great promise, not only for food addiction, but also for tobacco, alcohol, and drug addictions. If you just can't seem to get rid of an addiction problem, write in care of the publisher and we will send you information about this new technology.

THE NUTRITION AND DISEASE LINK

Nutrition plays an extremely important role in a number of disease states common in our society. There is progressively more information available about the link between eating and disease, and you should know much of this information as you attempt to keep yourself healthy and happy. The information on nutrition and disease that follows is not intended to give a complete description of these diseases or their treatment, but only to provide a few interesting and pertinent points. This information is not intended to take the place of medical advice. Any change in your diet or exercise patterns should be first cleared with your own physician, since your physician knows your individual history and needs.

OBESITY - For hundreds of years, excessive body fat was thought to be simply the result of excessive food intake; the extra calories, it was believed, were stored as fat. Overweight people were thought to be simply formerly thin people who had eaten too much, and who could be returned to their former thin state merely by cutting back their calories and thus burning off their extra fat stores to supply their energy needs.

In recent years, it has become apparent that this concept is totally erroneous. Many studies have clearly demonstrated that the average overweight person eats no more than, and in many cases considerably less than, the average thin person.[27,28,29,30] Body weight is now known to be closely regulated by control centers within the brain, which direct a number of metabolic processes to keep the weight at the "setpoint" level.[31] Many thin people consistently eat more than they need, and the control centers merely trigger energy-wasting systems which burn off the extra calories rather than storing them as fat.

Those who try to lose weight by reducing their caloric intake trigger various energy-conservation mechanisms which eventually slow down the metabolism and protect the fat stores.[32] Although some weight can be lost at first, soon even rigid dieting causes little or no weight loss. Fat storage enzymes are stimulated by restrictive eating, and as soon as anywhere near normal eating resumes, the fat is gained back many times faster than it would have been before dieting began.[33] In response to the perceived starvation, the setpoint goes up and the body typically gains more fat than ever in an apparent attempt to better protect against the next episode of starvation.[34]

Reduced-calorie dieting not only doesn't work, but actually may make you fatter than ever. In addition, dieting and the starvation defenses it triggers is associated with excessive hunger (especially for high-fat and high-sugar foods), preoccupation with food, fatigue, weakness, coldness, irritability, anxiety, depression, and a wide range of other problems.[35]

There are significant metabolic differences between obese people and thin people. Although some of these may be genetic, a number of them are acquired, especially through repeated calorie-reduced dieting and malnourishment from unhealthy eating. One of these major problems is that most overweight people are insulin-resistant and have higher levels of blood insulin than do thin people.[36] When your cells are resistant to the effects of insulin, it takes more insulin to get the sugar into the cells. These higher levels of insulin directly cause more fat to be produced and stored in your fat cells. If this insulin problem gets worse, diabetes eventually develops.

Obese people may also have impairment in the cell membrane transport systems which regulate the potassium and sodium balance within the cells.[37] A defect in the enzymes regulating cell transport of minerals, and also insulin resistance, may be secondary to a deficiency or imbalance in a number of minerals and, possibly, vitamins. For example, lack of potassium, calcium, magnesium, chromium, manganese, and zinc have all been shown to contribute to insulin resistance.

Although most of these minerals are present in adequate amounts in a balanced diet of unrefined foods, the average American diet is likely to be deficient in a number of these essential nutrients. Overweight people who frequently limit their caloric intake may develop progressively greater nutrient deficiencies. If their episodes of restrictive eating are alternated with periods of eating out of control (especially high-fat and high-sugar foods), then both the nutritional deficiencies and the obesity itself are made worse.

Now that we understand a great deal more about obesity and its causes, we can treat it much more effectively. In 1983, Garth Fisher, Ph.D., Edward Parent, Ph.D., and I published a book entitled *How to Lower Your Fat Thermostat*[38] which explained these new concepts. It outlined a program to take advantage of these new ideas. It explains how people can lose weight naturally and comfortably by doing the right things to lower the level at which their brains "choose" to regulate fat stores. Additional motivational and self-help guidelines are contained in Sybervision's audiotape program entitled *Neuropsychology of Weight Control*. This widely advertised program introduces some new concepts of learning and changing behavior, using the latest neuropsychological principles.

Some of the more important principles for this revolutionary new approach to weight loss are:

1. Eat enough food on a regular basis to completely satisfy your hunger. This is an important step in shutting off various starvation defenses and in creating a healthy brain chemical balance to promote a sense of contentment, happiness, relaxation, and well being.

2. Reduce the consumption of refined carbohydrates and sugar. This also includes avoiding any highly sweetened foods, including, of course, artificial sweeteners. For those who are addicted to sugar, artificial sweeteners, caffeine, or chocolate, breaking the addictive cycle is also very important. People with addictions should avoid the addictive foods completely for many months, and then should use them only occasionally after that. Keep in mind that even the occasional use can trigger a strong drive for these items and can keep the addiction cycle going. It is also easy to gradually increase the use of these foods until the old addictive pattern is right back again.

3. Reduce the consumption of fat in your diet. Most overweight people need to keep their fat intake down to between 10 and 20 percent of their total caloric intake. Both the book *How to Lower Your Fat Thermostat* and the tape series *Neuropsychology of Weight Control* have tables which list the composition of each major food item so that you can better adjust your diet.

4. Exercise at a moderate level on a regular basis.

DIABETES - There are two distinct types of diabetes mellitus. Type 1 is a condition in which inadequate amounts of insulin are produced to handle the sugar from your diet, leading to high levels of blood sugar. Type 2 diabetes is associated with insulin resistance; and even though higher-than-usual levels of insulin may be present, there is still excessive sugar in the bloodstream. Type 1 needs to be treated with insulin, but Type 2 can often be treated with more conservative measures.

The old approach to treatment of either type of diabetes was to greatly limit the amount of carbohydrate (since it can easily be converted to sugar) and to increase the amount of fat and protein. In more recent years, it has been discovered that this type of diet may be a major factor in the vascular problems associated with diabetes. Now, most experts are recommending diets lower in fat and protein, and with an increased amount of complex carbohydrate food.

Some attempt has been made to measure the speed with which various foods are processed and enter the bloodstream. Foods which are broken down quickly have been thought to be not as good for diabetics as those foods which break down over a longer period of time. Surprisingly, some vegetables and grains are processed almost as quickly as sucrose, and some experts have taught that because of this, sucrose may not be as bad for diabetics as previously thought, and could possibly be used by them in moderation.

In my opinion, there are at least four major reasons why diabetics (especially Type 2 diabetics) should carefully avoid the use of table sugar:

1. Sucrose use has been associated with weight gain, even though no extra calories are consumed.

2. Sucrose and other highly sweetened foods may interfere with the normal cephalic phase of insulin release leading to more weight gain and worsening of the diabetic state.

3. Type 2 diabetes, at least in part, appears to be a nutritional deficiency state, especially a result of the lack of a number of minerals. Sucrose has absolutely no minerals or vitamins, and the use of sucrose in place of unprocessed foods which do contain nutrients may further aggravate the problem.

4. Sucrose use has been shown to cause humans to excrete calcium and magnesium into the urine.[39] If diabetics use sugar, not only are they depriving themselves of important nutrients, but it may cause them to lose the limited stores of minerals which they do have.

Weight loss is very important for Type 2 diabetics who are overweight. Although the standard calorie-restricted diets usually cause weight loss and improve the diabetic picture on the short term, it is my observation on hundreds of diabetic patients that in the long term, this approach usually makes them fatter and worsens the diabetic state.

The recipes in this book are ideally suited for all diabetics, whether overweight or too thin, and whether they are Type 1 or Type 2 diabetics. For an overweight diabetic, the weight-loss program outlined in *How to Lower Your Fat Thermostat* is ideal. Both the Fat Thermostat program and the recipes in this book encourage plenty of good, nutritious food ideally suited for diabetics, which should help restore some of the deficient nutrients. The weight loss occurs naturally and comfortably. The exercise recommended is ideally suited for diabetes. In fact, many experts have pointed out that **exercise may be the single most important control measure for treating Type 2 diabetes.** Besides helping with the weight loss, exercise makes some profound changes in the insulin resistance, and does a great deal to restore normal blood sugar levels.

Most experts also agree that diabetic patients are very unlikely to stay with an exercise program for any length of time. This is probably because these experts have recommended that overweight diabetics also reduce their caloric intake at the same time. It is my firm conviction that **reduced-caloric intakes are completely incompatible with effective exercise.** The metabolic responses to reduced food intake make most people tired, and interferes with their ability to generate enough energy to sustain exercise for any period of time. They thus seldom develop the level of fitness needed to most effectively decrease the insulin resistance or lower the setpoint. The weakness and unpleasant feeling associated with the combination of exercise and restricted food intake makes exercise a very unpleasant experience for most people.

The combination of exercise and plenty of good, nutritious food is an entirely different situation. With adequate food intake, exercise will usually become a very pleasant experience associated with a feeling of vigor, increased energy, and an enhanced feeling of well being. With ample food, the fitness level goes up effectively in response to exercise, and various desirable metabolic changes associated with exercise seem to occur more readily.

HYPERTENSION - High blood pressure (hypertension) may also be a nutritional deficiency state. A number of studies with large populations have compared the diet of those with hypertension to those with normal blood pressure. Most of these studies have shown people with hypertension to be ingesting fewer calories, less fiber, less carbohydrate, and less calcium, magnesium, and potassium than those with normal blood pressure.[40,41,42,43] Other studies have shown that adding some of these nutrients will lower the blood pressure.[44,45,46,47]

A number of studies have shown that high blood pressure can be caused in several species of animals merely by alternating restricted food intake with refeeding.[48,49,50] After repeating this procedure several times, these experimental animals become hypertensive. It has also been shown that restricted food intake contributes to hypertension in humans.[51,52,53]

There appears to be a strong relationship between hypertension, diabetes, and obesity. These three conditions often seem to be found in the same patients, and the cell membrane defects may be the same. Certainly effective dietary management is much the same for all three conditions.

Of particular importance in treating hypertension is strict reduction in salt intake, even in those who don't have a short-term response to moderate salt restriction. The addition of high-potassium foods, and especially using healthier cooking techniques which preserve the potassium, are also important. Because of their low salt levels and their high mineral levels, the recipes in this book are ideally suited for the diet of someone with hypertension.

HIGH CHOLESTEROL - There is increasingly strong evidence that high serum cholesterol is a strong contributing factor for arteriosclerosis, leading to heart attacks and strokes. For every percentage point that the cholesterol is lowered, the risk of heart attack is lowered by 2 percent. Even the most strict restriction of cholesterol in the diet often makes only a slight to moderate reduction in cholesterol levels. Cholesterol can be manufactured by your own body, and there appears to be much more to the levels in your serum than the amount of cholesterol that you consume. Weight loss and exercise have also been shown to be effective cholesterol-lowering measures.

A few factors which are not as well known may also be of importance. An interesting study in Britain showed that those eating only one meal daily had significantly higher levels of cholesterol than those that ate three or more meals. Refined sugars seems to raise cholesterol levels for some people.

As with other health problems, nutritional deficiencies may play a role in high serum cholesterol levels. Recent studies have shown that magnesium can lower serum cholesterol, and can dramatically reduce the tendency of a high-cholesterol diet to cause arteriosclerosis.

There is likely to be a number of other dietary factors involved with cholesterol levels. Primitive societies consistently have much lower levels of serum cholesterol than those living in the western world. It is likely that a number of nutritional factors will soon be found which will explain these differences. In the meantime, a healthy, well-balanced diet with adequate nutrients and low in animal fats and cholesterol appears to be the best option for those with high cholesterol. Eating regular meals and exercise may also be helpful.

The recipes included in this book are all low in cholesterol and animal fats, and are well suited for treating this condition. (One exception is the conventional pie crust included with the sugar-free pies. Anyone with a cholesterol problem would do better to use the alternative, healthier options described for those recipes.) A number of recipes include oat bran, which has been shown to have a unique action in lowering cholesterol.

HEART DISEASE, STROKES, AND ARTERIOSCLEROSIS - There has been a great deal of recent research to identify the causes of arteriosclerosis (hardening of the arteries) which leads to so many serious health problems and deaths in our society. Besides the role played by heredity, smoking, obesity, inactivity, and high blood pressure, there appears to be a number of dietary factors involved.

A number of population studies have been done in which the diets of thousands of people were analyzed; the diet of those with heart disease or strokes were compared with those who did not have these problems. One study involved 8,218 Puerto Rican men,[54] one involved 7,705 Japanese men living in Hawaii,[55] and another study compared men living in Boston to their brothers living in Ireland.[56] In all of these studies, some surprising results surfaced. Those who developed heart attacks or died from heart disease consistently ate fewer calories, less carbohydrate, and less fiber than those who didn't have heart disease. A number of these researchers pointed out the protective effect of eating larger amounts of food from plant sources.

In these studies, the relationship of dietary fats and cholesterol to arteriosclerosis was not nearly as strong as was its relationship to lower caloric intake, lower carbohydrate intake, and less fiber consumption. There was usually not much difference between the total amount of fats and cholesterol consumed, but those with the health problems ate a higher percentage of their total calories in the form of fat (since they ate fewer total calories) than those who were healthy.

The recipes in this book are ideally suited for those who wish to keep their fat intake down to treat or prevent arteriosclerosis. Even more important, they contain high levels of complex carbohydrates with their protective fiber, calories, and other nutrients.

OSTEOPOROSIS - Loss of minerals from the bones, weakening them and making them more vulnerable to fractures and disintegration, has become a virtual epidemic in our society. It has been long taught that this condition is a result of deficiency in dietary calcium. Several lines of logic question this concept. Members of other societies eating more basic foods and less calcium than we eat suffer very little osteoporosis. Adding calcium to the diet has not been shown to reverse the loss of bones.[57]

One new study pointed out that those using sucrose in their diets lost calcium and magnesium in their urine. In fact, they lost more of these minerals than they were ingesting, suggesting that some of it was broken down from the bones or other mineral stores. Since the average person ingests about 125 pounds of sugar yearly, this could contribute to significant loss of minerals from the bones. Certainly further research is needed, but this could prove to be a much more important contributor to osteoporosis that the other suspected factors.

When you eat a diet high in sugar, you are typically depriving yourself of the mineral- and vitamin-containing foods you would otherwise eat. Keep in mind that absorption and utilization of calcium and magnesium requires vitamin D and a number of other nutrients. Lack of some of these nutrients may also prove to play a role in osteoporosis.

With the information we now have, it certainly makes sense to prevent osteoporosis by eating plenty of unrefined foods high in minerals and vitamins, avoiding excessive sucrose, and exercising on a regular basis. Because the recipes in this book contain no refined sugar, and have plenty of unprocessed foods high in nutrients, they may be useful for those concerned about this increasingly common problem.

PREMENSTRUAL SYNDROME (PMS) - A great deal of attention in the lay literature has recently been focused on the problem of unpleasant symptoms occurring before the onset of menstruation. In some cases, these symptoms can be very severe and extremely debilitating and disruptive. Although no single cause has been isolated as **the cause** of PMS, a few dietary factors have been identified. Most researchers have recognized that avoidance of sugar and caffeine is helpful. Certain nutrients have been shown in double-blind studies to also be helpful (including vitamin B6, vitamin E, magnesium, and some types of fatty acids). This would suggest a possible deficiency of these nutrients in the diets of those with PMS.

It has certainly been our experience that those with PMS who improve their diet and exercise on a regular basis significantly decrease their symptoms.

A number of writers have also noted the relationship between sugar intake and menstrual cramps. It has been our experience also that those who stop using refined sugar often notice a remarkable improvement in menstrual cramps.

The recipes in this book should be an excellent alternative for the women who usually give in to strong sugar cravings before their periods and then feel worse. These recipes should taste very good to them, and help treat the problem instead of aggravating it.

CANCER - Experts now believe that many types of cancers are related to our diets and habits. A study in Greece analyzed the diets of 240 women.[58] They were divided into five groups according to the number of vegetables that they consumed. The group consuming the fewest amount of vegetables had a breast cancer rate ten times that of the group consuming the most vegetables. A number of other studies have also confirmed the protective nature of eating vegetables and fresh fruit.[59,60] Some scientists have suggested a protective role of the vitamin C, Vitamin E, and vitamin A that these foods contain. One scientist has studied hundreds of natural chemical substances found within various foods, and has given evidence that there are a number of food chemicals which protect against the development of certain types of cancer.[61] Some of these chemicals may even counteract the effect of known cancer inducing chemicals, such as tobacco smoke and charred meat.

Diets high in fat content have been associated with a higher than average risk of some types of cancer.[62] Fats refined from plant sources seem to more likely than animals fats to be cancer-causing.[63] This could be because animal fats like butter and cream contain some of the fat-soluble vitamins thought to play a cancer-protective role.

The recipes in this book contain unrefined foods which contain many of the food chemicals thought to be protective against cancers. They also are low in fat. The fruit and fruit juice concentrates used in a lot of these recipes contain protective vitamins.

INFECTIONS AND IMMUNITY - Those of us who work closely with patients making various dietary changes are aware of a strong relationship between dietary deficiencies and susceptibility to infections.[64] Before we had better techniques, I used to closely supervise hundreds of people on very restrictive diets. After a few weeks, it seemed like a lot of these people developed colds, flu, or other infections at a higher rate than one would expect. In taking a close history of those who have developed chronic virus infections, many patients describe eating a very poor diet, being under stress, missing sleep, and then developing a bad infection (like mononucleosis) which then never goes away completely.

Scientists have now demonstrated that a number of vitamins reduce the risk of developing infection. Vitamin C has been associated with a reduced risk of developing colds, and when taken in high doses, may decrease the severity and duration of a cold. A study in Africa among malnourished children showed that giving just one high-potency vitamin A capsule every six months reduced the death rate from infection by an incredible 70 percent,[65] and this is just one of many vitamins necessary for good immunity.

Much interest has focused recently on why some people who have been exposed to the virus which causes AIDS develop AIDS and die, and why others don't seem to become ill. One study suggested that those who don't become ill are ingesting more zinc, which may bolster immunity,[66] than the other group.

In our medical office, we deal with a lot of people with chronic infections, or people who develop repeated infections like sinus, urinary tract, vaginal, or throat infections. A healthier diet often greatly reduces the recurrence rate of these infections, and reduces the severity of the symptoms associated with chronic infections. Many of these patients with improved resistance have reported indulging in various sweets over a holiday and within hours developing a nasty infection again, just like they used to before improving their diets.

People with immune system concerns should be able to enjoy the desserts and treats in this book without worrying about negative effects on their health.

SUGGESTIONS FOR USING THE RECIPES

All of the health problems discussed above are at least partly the result of inadequate nutrient intake. **It makes no sense at all for people to continue treating these nutritional deficiency states with diets which impair their nutritional status even further.** It is my opinion that too much time and effort is spent convincing people to cut back on problem foods and total calories. Not enough emphasis is placed on encouraging them to eat plenty of nutritious, protective foods. Not enough suggestions are given to help people develop a healthier diet and lifestyle.

Besides providing our biological needs for energy and nutrients, eating plays a number of other important roles in our society. Bonds of love and closeness between family members and friends are often strengthened by eating together and by giving each other food gifts. Some families never get together except to share a meal, and this may be the only time that they communicate and interact with each other. Mothers or other family members who feel that they can't eat the food served to the other members, and who stay away from the table to avoid temptation, are deprived of the association with and support of their family.

This recipe book should be a tremendous help to those who are trying to juggle the problems of improving their own and their families' diets, and yet keeping the fun, enjoyment, and other benefits associated with eating together. These recipes are ideal for parties, picnics, family dinners, and for treats to serve your family. If you don't tell kids that these are healthy foods, they are unlikely to know the difference.

Although the recipes in this book are much more nutritious than usual recipes of this type, keep in mind that a good balanced diet is important for good health. One cannot live just on these desserts, excluding fresh vegetables from their diet, and expect to experience optimal health. Barbara and I are convinced that children should not have free access to highly sweetened food and drink, even the healthy desserts and snacks in this book. Balanced meals should be served on a regular basis, and the dessert and treat items in this book should be used in addition to healthy meals, not as a replacement for them.

As you continue to avoid refined sugars and artificial sweeteners, your tastes should change enough that even the least sweet of these recipes will taste delicious.

We encourage you to try many of these recipes, but don't repeat only the very sweetest tasting of them. Use a variety! We are concerned that for some people, the sweeter recipes may continue to trigger the desire for more sweet foods and may interfere with their desire for and enjoyment of foods such as vegetables and whole-grain products. If you feel that this is a problem for you, then avoid the sweetest recipes, but enjoy the other ones. Some recipes have some alternatives. As you begin to enjoy foods with less sweetness, you may want to use the options that are not quite as sweet, especially if you are concerned about your weight.

Each recipe has information about diabetic exchanges, making it easier for people with diabetes to fit these recipes into their diets.

Each recipe has been analyzed, and nutritional information is provided which may be useful. The various designations are used in our books *How to Lower Your Fat Thermostat*, *Recipes to Lower Your Fat Thermostat*, and in Sybervision's *Neuropsychology of Weight Control* tape series. These designations are of little value unless you have the original book which explains the point system.

This nutritional information will hopefully help you become more aware of what you are eating and the comparison between different foods.

I am excited about the potential that this book has for maintaining the enjoyment and advantages of eating together, and yet providing healthy, delicious foods for everyone, regardless of their health problems. It is my hope that you enjoy these recipes and that you find great enjoyment, satisfaction, and health benefits from eating a healthy diet. I wish you good health and happy eating!

1. American Cancer Society. Cancer Prevention Study II, An epidemiological study of lifestyle and environment. CPS II Newsletter. Spring, 1986;4/1:3.

2. Blundell JE, Hill AJ. Paradoxical effects of an intense sweetener (aspartame) on appetite. Lancet May 10, 1986;pp.1092-93.

3. Committee for a Study on Saccharin and Food Safety Policy: Saccharin: Technical Assessment of Risks and Benefits (Report No. 1). Washington, DC, Assembly of Life Sciences/Institute of Medicine, National Research Council/National Academy of Sciences, 1978.

4. Cohen SM, Arai M, Jacobs JB, et al. Promoting effects of saccharin and DL tryptophan in urinary bladder carcinogenesis. Cancer Res 1979;39:1207-17.

5. Remington DW, Higa B. The Bitter Truth About Artificial Sweeteners. Provo, UT: Vitality House International Inc.,1987.

6. Hunt JC: Sodium intake and hypertension: A cause for concern. Ann Intern Med 1983;98:724-28.

7. Houston MC. Sodium and Hypertension: A review. Arch Intern Med 1986;146:179-85.

8. Connor SL, Gustafson JR, Artaud-Wild SM, Flavell DP, Classick-Kohn CJ, Hatcher LF, Connor WE. The Cholesterol/Saturated-Fat Index: An indication of the hypercholesterolaemic and atherogenic potential of food. The Lancet May 31, 1986:1229-32.

9. Root RK. Diet and Cancer - Should We Change What We Eat? West J Med 1987;146.1:73-8.

10. Kromhout D, Bosschieter EB, Coulander CL. The inverse relation between fish consumption and 20-year mortality from coronary heart disease. N Engl J Med 1985;312:1205-9.

11. Davis CM. Results of the self-selection of diets by young children. Can Med Assoc J 1939;41:257-61.

12. Story M, Brown JE. Do young children instinctively know what to eat? N Engl J Med 1987;312:103-5.

13. Sclafani A. Feeding inhibition and death produced by glucose ingestion in the rat. Physiol Behav 1973;11:595-601.

14. Berhoud HR, Bereiter DA, Trimble E, Siegel EG, Jeanrenaud B. Cephalic phase, reflex insulin secretion. Diabetologia 1981;20:393-401.

15. von Borstel RW. Metabolic and physiologic effects of sweeteners. Clin Nutr 1985;4/6:217-20.

16. Raymond CA. Obesity many disorders: causes sought in genes, neurochemistry, psychology. JAMA 1986;256:2301.

17. MacKay EM, Calloway JW, Barnes RH. Hyperalimentation in normal animals produced by protamine insulin. J Nutr 1940;20:59-66.

18. Hoebel BG, Teitelbaum P. Weight regulation in normal and hypothalamic hyperphagic rates. J Comp Physiol Psychol 1966;61:89-93.

19. Powley TL. The ventromedial hypothalamic syndrome, satiety, and a cephalic phase hypothesis. Psychol Review 1977;84/1:90.

20. Kanarek RB, Hirsch E. Developmental aspects of sucrose-induced obesity in rats. Physiol Behav 1979;23:881-85.

21. Sclafani A, Xenakis S. Sucrose and polysaccharide induced obesity in the rat. Physiol Behav 1984;32:169-74.

22. Grossman MI. Pancreatic secretion in the rat. Am J Physiol 1958;194:535-39.

23. Leveille GA. Adipose tissue metabolism: Influence of periodicity of eating and diet composition. Fed Proc 1970;29:1294-1301.

24. Deutsch R. Conditioned hypoglycemia: a mechanism for saccharin-induced sensitivity to insulin in the rat. J Compartive Physiol Psychol 1974;86/2:350-58.

25. Louis-Sylvestre J. Preabsorptive insulin release and hypogylcemia in rats. Am J Physiol 1976;230/1:59.

26. Wadden T. Presentation to the American Society of Bariatric Physicians at Reno, Nevada. October 1983

27. Wooley SC, Wooley OW, Dyrenforth SR. Theoretical, practical and social issues in behavioral treatments of obesity. J Appl Behav Analy 1979;12:3-25.

28. Keen H, Thomas BJ, Jarrett RJ, Fuller JH. Nutrient intake, adiposity and diabetes. Br Med J 1979;1:655-58.

29. Kromhout D. Energy and macronutrient intake in lean and obese middle-aged men (the Zutphen Study). Am J Clin Nutr 1983;37:295-99.

30. Johnson ML, Burke BS, Mayer J. The prevalence and incidence of obesity in a cross-section of elementary school children. Am J Clin Nutr 1959;7:55-62.

31. Bernardis LL, McEwen G, Kodis M. Body weight set point studies in weanling rats with dorsomedial hypothalamic lesions (DMNL Rats). Brain Research Bulletin 1986;17:451-60.

32. Boyle PC, Storlein H, Keesey RE. Increased efficiency of food utilization following weight loss. Physiol Behav 1978;21:261-64.

33. Greenwood MRC, Cleary M, et al. Adipose tissue metabolism and genetic obesity: the LPL hypothesis. In: Recent Advances in Obesity Research: III. Eds: Bjorntorp P, Cairella M, Howard AN. London, Eng: John Libbey, 1981; pp.75-79.

34. Schwartz RS, Brunzell JD. Adipose tissue lipoprotein lipase and obesity. In: Recent Advances In Obesity Research: III. Eds: Bjorntorp P, Cairella M, Howard AN. London, Eng: John Libbey, 1981:pp.94-97.

35. Keys A, Brozek J, et al. The Biology of Human Starvation. Vol. 1. Minneapolis, MN: University of Minnesota Press, 1950.

36. Jequier E, Schutz Y. Does a defect in energy metabolism contribute to human obesity? In:Recent Advances in Obesity Research:IV. Eds: Hirsch J, Van Itallie TB. London, Eng: John Libbey, 1983;pp.76-81.

37. Belfiore F, Iannello S, Rabuazzo AM, Borzi V. The activity of sodium and potassium-activated adenosine-triphosphatase (NaK-ATPase) in the adipose tissue of obese patients. In: Obesity: Pathogenesis and Treatment. Eds: Enzi G, Crepaldi G, Pozza G, Renold AE. London, New York, Toronto, Sydney, San Fransisco. Academic Press, 1981:pp.129-34.

38. Remington DW, Fisher GA, Parent EA. How To Lower Your Fat Thermostat. Provo, UT. Vitality House International, Inc., 1983.

39. Gonzale-Calvin JL, et al. Efectos de la ingestion de sacarosa sobre la diuresis, calciuria y otros constituyentes urinarios en sujetos sanos. Rev Clin Esp 1981;160:293-97.

40. Wright A, Burstyn PG, Gibney MJ. Dietary fibre and blood pressure. Brit Med J 1979;2:1541-43.

41. Khaw KT, Barret-Conor E. Dietary potassium and blood pressure in a population. Am J Clin Nutr 1984;39:963-68.

42. Kromout D, Bosschieter EB, Coulander CL. Potassium, calcium, alcohol intake and blood pressure: the Zutphen Study. Am J Clin Nutr 1985;41:1299-1304.

43. McCarron DA, Morris CD, et al. Blood pressure and nutrient intake in the United States. Science 1984;224:1392-98.

44. Weinsier RL, Norris D. Recent developments in the etiology and treatment of hypertension: dietary calcium, fat, and magnesium. Am J Clin Nutr 1985;42:1331-38.

45. Lyle RM, Melby CL, Hyner GC, Edmondson JW, Miller JZ, Weinberger MH. Blood pressure and metabolic effects of calcium supplementation in normotensive white and black men. JAMA 1987;257:1772-76.

46. MacGregor GA, Smith SJ, Markandu ND, Banks RA, Sagnella GA. Moderate potassium supplementation in essential hypertension. Lancet Sept. 11, 1982:567-70.

47. Dyckner T, Wester PO. Effect of magnesium on blood pressure. Br Med J 1983;286:1847-49.

48. Ernsberger PR. Neural mediation of genetic and nutritional effects on blood pressure: role of adrenergic receptor regulation in the kidney, brain, and heart. A dissertation submitted to the graduate school in partial fulfillment of the requirements of the degree Doctor of Philosophy. Northwestern University. Ausust, 1984.

49. Wilhelmaj CM, Carnazzo AJ, McCarthy HH. Effect of fasting and realimentation with diets high in carbohydrate or protein on blood pressure and heart rate of sympathectomized dogs. Am J Physiol 1957;191:103-7.

50. Smith-Vaniz GT, Ashburn AD, Williams WL. Diet-induced hypertension and cardiovascular lesions in mice. The Yale Journal of Biology and Medicine. 1970;43:61-70.

51. Brozek J, Chapman CB, Keys A. Drastic food restriction; effect on cardiovascular dynamics in normotensive and hypertensive conditions. JAMA 1948;137:1569-74.

52. Harrison GF. Nutritional deficiency, painful feet, high blood pressure in Hong Kong. Lancet 1946;1:961-64.

53. Stapleton R. Edema in recovered prisoners of war. Lancet 1946;1:1850-51.

54. Garcia-Palmieri MR, Sorlie P, Tillotson J, Costas R, Cordero E, Rodriguez M. Relationship of dietary intake to subsequent coronary heart disease incidence: The Puerto Rico Heart Health Program. Am J Clin Nutr 1980;33:1818-27.

55. Yano K, Rhoads GG, Kagan A, Tillotson J. Dietary intake and the risk of coronary heart disease in Japanese men living in Hawaii. Am J Clin Nutr 1978;31:1270-79.

56. Kushi LH, Lew RA, Stare FJ, et al. Diet and 20-year mortality from coronary heart disease: The Ireland-Boston diet-heart study. N Eng J Med 1985;312:811-18.

57. Osteoporosis: Most answers yet to come. Science News 1987;131:116.

58.Katsouyanni K, Trichopoulos D, et al. Diet and breast cancer: a case-control study in Greece. Int J Cancer 1986;38:815-20.

59. Bjelke E. Epidemiologic studies of cancer of the stomach, colon, and rectum, with special emphasis on the role of diet. Vol. 3. Ann Arbor, MI: University Microfilm, 1973;pp.273-343.

60. Colditz GA, Branch LG, et al. Increased green and yellow vegetable intake and lowered cancer deaths in an elderly population. Am J Clin Nutr 1985;41:32-6.

61. Wong J. Cancer and chemicals...and vegetables. Chemtech July 1986:pps.436-43.

62. Willett WC, MacMahon B. Diet and cancer - and overview. N Eng J Med 1984;310:697-703.

63. Root RK. Diet and Cancer - should we change what we eat? West J Med 1987;146:73-78.

64. Chandra RK. Interactions of nutrition, infection and immune response. Acta Paediatrica Scandinavica 1979;68:137-44.

65. Raloff J. New benefits seen in vitamin A therapy. Science News May 23, 1987:pp.325.

66. Fabris N, Mocchegiani E, Galli M, Irato L, Lazzarin A, Moroni M. AIDS, Zinc deficiency, and thymic hormone failure. JAMA 1988;259:839-40.

Chapter One

Cookies

Cookies

Few aromas that come from the kitchen are as inviting as that of fresh cookies baking. A frosty glass of milk waiting for a warm cookie always spells fun. Wonderful traditions are created when parents and children bake cookies together. Remember how much fun you had helping Mom bake your favorite cookie recipe--and how anxious you were for the cookies to cool so you could savor that first moist bite?

You might think a change to healthier eating habits means no more cookie baking. After all, cookies are known for their high sugar and high fat content, certainly not conducive to good eating habits. In a regular cookie recipe, 35 to 52 percent--or more-- of the calories come from fat.

This chapter offers you an opportunity to keep baking cookies--but to do it within the framework of sound health principles. Cookie jars don't have to be a thing of the past. Now you can fill them with fresh-baked, great-tasting, healthy cookies. When the Cub Scouts call or the P.T.A. wants cookies, turn to this chapter and bake them something that not only tastes good, but is good for them.

AUNT ANNE'S SUGARLESS COOKIES

With just a few changes from Aunt Anne's original recipe, this great-tasting cookie will fool even sugar-lovers.

1	C	raisins
½	C	chopped dates
1	C	chopped apples, peeled and cored
1	C	frozen unsweetened pear-apple or apple concentrate, thawed
¼	C	margarine or butter, softened
2	lg	egg whites
1	tsp	vanilla
2	C	whole wheat flour
1	tsp	baking soda
1	C	quick-cooking rolled oats
½	C	chopped walnuts, optional

1. Boil raisins, dates, and apples in juice concentrate for 10 minutes. Add butter to hot mixture; let cool.

2. Place fruit mixture in mixing bowl. Add egg whites and vanilla; beat well.

3. Add flour, soda, and oats; beat well. Stir in nuts.

4. Drop by teaspoonfuls onto cookie sheet that has been sprayed with nonstick vegetable coating.

5. Bake in 350° oven for 12 minutes or until lightly golden brown on top.

Yield: 48 cookies

	RCU	FU	Cal	%Fat	P	F	C	Na
Per Cookie	0	0	59	18.5	1	1	11	32

3 Cookies = 1 Fruit exchange; 1 Bread exchange; 1/2 Fat exchange

MIXED FRUIT COOKIES

This recipe produces a soft, tasty cookie. Each cookie tastes slightly different, depending upon which combination of fruit from the Fruit Bits is scooped up.

3	T	cold-pressed oil
3	lg	egg whites
¾	C	frozen unsweetened apple juice concentrate, thawed
¼	C	frozen unsweetened pineapple-orange concentrate, thawed
2	C	whole wheat flour
1½	C	quick-cooking rolled oats
1	tsp	cinnamon
1	tsp	baking soda
½	C	chopped toasted almonds, optional
1	6-oz pkg.	Sun Maid Fruit Bits

1. Beat oil and egg whites until light.

2. Add juice concentrates and beat until blended.

3. Add flour, oats, baking soda, and cinnamon and beat until well blended.

4. Stir in almonds and Fruit Bits.

5. Place by teaspoonfuls onto cookie sheet. Bake for 10 minutes at 350°.

Yield: 4 dozen

	RCU	FU	Cal	%Fat	P	F	C	Na
Per Cookie	0	0	54	19	1	1	10	22

3 Cookies = 1 Fruit exchange; 1 Bread exchange; 1/2 Fat exchange

DATE NUT COOKIES

This soft, flavorful cookie is a favorite of all who taste it.

3	T	margarine or butter, softened
1	lg	egg white
3	oz.	frozen unsweetened pineapple juice concentrate, thawed
3	oz.	frozen unsweetened apple juice concentrate, thawed
2	tsp	vanilla
2	C	whole wheat flour
1	tsp	baking soda
1	C	chopped dates
½	C	chopped walnuts, optional

1. Cream margarine; add egg white, juice concentrates, and vanilla. Mix well.

2. Add flour and baking soda; mix until well blended.

3. Stir in dates and walnuts.

4. Drop by teaspoonfuls onto cookie sheets sprayed with nonstick vegetable coating.

5. Bake at 350° for 10 to 12 minutes.

Yield: 48 cookies

	RCU	FU	Cal	%Fat	P	F	C	Na
Per Cookie	0	0	41	18	1	1	8	27

3 Cookies = 1 Fruit exchange; 1/2 Bread exchange; 1/2 Fat exchange

APRICOT-DATE COOKIES

The apricots provide a unique taste to these delicious, tangy cookies.

¼	C	margarine or butter, softened
1	lg	egg white
½	C	frozen unsweetened orange juice concentrate, thawed
½	C	frozen unsweetened apple juice concentrate, thawed
1¼	C	whole wheat flour
1¼	C	quick-cooking rolled oats
1	tsp	baking soda
½	C	chopped dried apricots
½	C	chopped dates
½	C	raisins
⅓	C	chopped walnuts, optional

1. Combine butter, egg white, and juice concentrates; beat well.

2. Add flour, oats, and baking soda; beat until smooth.

3. Stir in apricots, dates, raisins, and walnuts.

4. Spray cookie sheet with nonstick vegetable coating. Drop dough by teaspoonfuls onto prepared cookie sheet.

5. Bake at 350° for 12 minutes, or until lightly brown.

Yield: 3 1/2 dozen

	RCU	FU	Cal	%Fat	P	F	C	Na
Per Cookie	0	0	57	21	1	1	11	35

2 Cookies = 1 Fruit exchange; 1/2 Bread exchange; 1/2 Fat exchange

BANANA-OATMEAL COOKIES

A great way to use those over-ripe bananas--the kids will love them!

2	C	whole wheat flour
¾	tsp	baking soda
1	tsp	cinnamon
½	tsp	nutmeg
¼	C	cold-pressed oil
¼	C	frozen unsweetened pineapple juice concentrate, thawed
¼	C	frozen unsweetened apple juice concentrate, thawed
2	lg	egg whites
1	C	mashed ripe bananas (about 3)
1	tsp	vanilla
2	C	quick-cooking rolled oats
½	C	chopped nuts (walnuts or pecans), optional

1. Combine oil, juice concentrates, egg whites, mashed bananas, and vanilla. Beat well.

2. Add flour, baking soda, cinnamon, and nutmeg. Mix well.

3. Stir in oats and chopped nuts.

4. Drop by rounded teaspoonfuls onto cookie sheets that have been sprayed with nonstick vegetable coating.

5. Bake at 350° for 10 to 12 minutes. When cookies are cool, place in a plastic bag. These cookies are better eaten the next day; the banana flavor ripens overnight.

Yield: 2 1/2 dozen cookies

	RCU	FU	Cal	%Fat	P	F	C	Na
Per Cookie	0	0	81	22	2	2	14	25

2 Cookies = 1/2 Fruit exchange; 1 Bread exchange; 1/2 Fat exchange

APPLE COOKIES

A mildly spicy cookie with an appealing taste.

2	T	cold-pressed oil
2	lg	egg whites
¾	C	frozen unsweetened apple juice concentrate, thawed
1½	C	whole wheat flour
1½	C	quick-cooking rolled oats
1	tsp	baking powder
1	tsp	cinnamon
¼	tsp	nutmeg
1	med	apple, peeled, cored, and finely diced
¼	C	raisins

1. Combine oil, egg whites, and apple juice concentrate; beat well.

2. Combine flour, oats, baking powder, cinnamon, and nutmeg; add to creamed mixture, mixing well.

3. Stir in diced apple and raisins.

4. Drop dough by rounded teaspoonfuls onto cookie sheets sprayed with nonstick vegetable coating.

5. Bake at 350° for 10 to 12 minutes.

Yield: 3 dozen cookies

	RCU	FU	Cal	%Fat	P	F	C	Na
Per Cookie	0	0	52	19	2	1	10	13

2 Cookies = 1/2 Fruit exchange; 1 Bread exchange

GRANOLA COOKIES

This cookie is sure to be a favorite of everyone you serve it to. The taste of this cookie--another great way to use your homemade granola (see recipe)--will depend upon what you add to your granola.

Need more liquid; w'3c + water

1	C	raisins
¾	C	frozen unsweetened apple juice concentrate, thawed
3	T	cold-pressed oil
2	lg	egg whites
1½	C	whole wheat flour
1	tsp	baking soda
½	tsp	cinnamon
¼	tsp	finely grated orange peel
2	C	granola (see recipe chapter 9)

1. Soak raisins in apple juice concentrate.

2. Beat oil and egg whites until light.

3. Add raisin-apple juice mixture.

4. Add flour, baking soda, cinnamon, orange peel, and granola; stir until well combined.

5. Place by teaspoonfuls on cookie sheet. Bake for 8 to 10 minutes at 350°.

Yield: 4 dozen

	RCU	FU	Cal	%Fat	P	F	C	Na
Per Cookie	0	0	54	24	1	1.5	10	29

4 Cookies = 1 Fruit exchange; 1 Bread exchange; 1 Fat exchange

APPLE AND DATE COOKIES

A good-tasting soft cookie; you won't even miss the sugar!

3	T	margarine or butter, softened
1	lg	egg white
1	tsp	vanilla
¾	C	frozen unsweetened apple juice concentrate, thawed
1	C	whole wheat flour
½	tsp	baking soda
½	tsp	cinnamon
¼	tsp	ground ginger
⅛	tsp	nutmeg
1	C	quick-cooking rolled oats
½	C	Red Delicious apple, grated, peeled, and cored
⅓	C	chopped dates

1. Cream butter; add egg white and vanilla. Beat well.

2. Add apple juice concentrate and beat well.

3. Combine flour, soda, cinnamon, ginger, and nutmeg; add to the creamed mixture.

4. Stir in oats, apple, and dates.

5. Drop dough by rounded teaspoonfuls onto cookie sheets sprayed with nonstick vegetable cooking.

6. Bake at 350° for 12 minutes.

Yield: 32 cookies

	RCU	FU	Cal	%Fat	P	F	C	Na
Per Cookie	0	0	51	24	1	1	9	27

4 Cookies = 1 Fruit exchange; 1 Bread exchange; 1 Fat exchange

RAISIN SPICE COOKIES

Sure to be a favorite of those who enjoy spicy cookies.

2	C	raisins
1	lg	egg white
1	C	frozen unsweetened apple juice concentrate, thawed
3	T	margarine or butter, softened
1	C	quick-cooking rolled oats
1½	C	whole wheat flour
1	tsp	baking soda
1	tsp	cinnamon
1	tsp	ground cloves
¼	C	raisin water

1. Place raisins in saucepan and cover with water; boil for 10 minutes. Drain well and save the water.

2. Mix egg white, apple juice concentrate, and margarine.

3. Add flour, soda, cinnamon, and cloves; mix well.

4. Add 1/4 cup of reserved raisin water.

5. Place by teaspoonfuls onto cookie sheet that has been sprayed with nonstick vegetable coating.

6. Bake at 350° for 10 minutes, or until lightly brown.

Yield: 3 1/2 dozen cookies

	RCU	FU	Cal	%Fat	P	F	C	Na
Per Cookie	0	0	64	19	1	1	13	36

2 Cookies = 1 Fruit exchange; 1/2 Bread exchange; 1/2 Fat exchange

PINEAPPLE CARROT COOKIES

The kids will never know that this tasty, soft cookie has carrots in it.

3	T	margarine or butter, softened
1	lg	egg white
¼	C	frozen unsweetened apple juice concentrate, thawed
½	C	frozen unsweetened pineapple juice concentrate, thawed
½	tsp	vanilla
2	C	whole wheat flour
1½	tsp	baking soda
1½	tsp	cinnamon
¾	tsp	nutmeg
1	tsp	ginger
¾	C	unsweetened crushed pineapple, drained well
1	C	finely grated carrots
¾	C	quick-cooking rolled oats
⅓	C	currants

1. Cream softened butter and add egg white; beat well.

2. Add vanilla and juice concentrates; beat well.

3. Combine flour, baking soda, cinnamon, nutmeg, and ginger; add to the butter mixture.

4. Stir in oats, pineapple, carrots, and currants; mix until well blended.

5. Drop dough by rounded teaspoonfuls onto cookie sheets sprayed with nonstick vegetable coating. Bake at 350° for 10 to 12 minutes.

Yield: 48 cookies

	RCU	FU	Cal	%Fat	P	F	C	Na
Per Cookie	0	0	42	19.9	1	1	8	37

3 Cookies = 1/2 Fruit exchange; 1 Bread exchange; 1/2 Fat exchange

FRUIT BARS

A quick and easy way to make cookies with no added oil.

1	C	unsweetened apple juice concentrate, thawed
1	med	banana
1	lg	egg white
½	tsp	lemon extract
1	tsp	vanilla
½	C	oat bran
1	C	quick-cooking rolled oats
¾	C	whole wheat flour
2	tsp	baking powder
½	tsp	cinnamon
⅓	C	chopped dates
⅓	C	chopped walnuts, optional

1. Combine apple concentrate, banana, egg white, lemon extract, and vanilla extract in a mixing bowl; beat until smooth.

2. Add oat bran, oats, flour, baking powder, and cinnamon; mix until smooth.

3. Stir in dates and nuts.

4. Pour into a 9" x 9" pan that has been sprayed with nonstick vegetable coating.

5. Bake at 350° for 25 minutes.

Yield: 12 bars

	RCU	FU	Cal	%Fat	P	F	C	Na
Per Bar	0	0	132	7	3	1	29	63

1 Bar = 1 Fruit exchange; 1 Bread exchange

RAISIN SPICE SQUARES

Bar cookies are a quick and easy way to make a treat.

1	C	raisins
1	C	unsweetened apple juice concentrate, thawed
3	T	cold-pressed oil
2	lg	egg whites
1	tsp	vanilla
1¾	C	whole wheat flour
¼	C	wheat germ
1	tsp	baking soda
1	tsp	baking powder
1	tsp	cinnamon
⅛	tsp	nutmeg
⅛	tsp	allspice
⅛	tsp	ground cloves
¼	C	chopped walnuts, optional

1. Mix together raisins and apple juice concentrate in a small saucepan; bring to a boil.

2. Combine oil, egg whites, and vanilla; beat well. Add raisin mixture; blend well.

3. Add dry ingredients and mix until well blended. Add nuts.

4. Spray 9" x 9" baking pan with nonstick vegetable coating. Pour batter into the pan and bake at 375° for 25 minutes. Cut into squares when cool.

Yield: 16 squares (one per serving)

	RCU	FU	Cal	%Fat	P	F	C	Na
Per Square	0	0	133	21	3	3	25	83

1 Square = 1 Fruit exchange; 1/2 Bread exchange; 1/2 Fat exchange

FRUIT SQUARES

A moist, flavorful, easy-to-prepare cookie.

1	lg	apple, peeled, cored, and grated (about 1 cup)
1	med	ripe banana, mashed (about 1/2 cup)
½	C	frozen unsweetened apple juice concentrate, thawed
1	lg	egg white
1½	tsp	vanilla
1¼	C	whole wheat flour
¼	C	quick-cooking rolled oats
1	tsp	cinnamon
½	tsp	baking soda
½	C	raisins

1. Heat oven to 350°.

2. Spray an 8" x 8" baking pan with nonstick vegetable coating.

3. In a large bowl, beat grated apple, banana, apple juice, egg white, and vanilla until well blended.

4. At a low speed, beat in flour, oats, cinnamon, and baking soda to blend.

5. Stir in raisins. Spoon batter into prepared pan; bake 25 to 30 minutes.

Yield: 16 squares

	RCU	FU	Cal	%Fat	P	F	C	Na
Per Square	0	0	83	4	2	T	19	32

1 Square = 1/2 Fruit exchange; 1/2 Bread exchange

PUMPKIN BARS

Serve warm or cold for a tasty fall treat--a fun way to use pumpkin.

3	T	cold-pressed oil
1	lg	egg white
1	tsp	vanilla
1	C	canned pumpkin
1	C	frozen unsweetened apple juice concentrate, thawed
2	C	whole wheat flour
1	C	quick-cooking rolled oats
1	tsp	baking soda
1	tsp	cinnamon
½	C	golden raisins

1. Beat together oil and egg white. Add vanilla and pumpkin, and blend well.

2. Blend in apple juice concentrate.

3. Add flour, oats, soda, and cinnamon. Mix well.

4. Stir in raisins.

5. Pour into 7" x 11" baking pan that has been sprayed with nonstick vegetable coating.

6. Bake at 375° for 20 to 25 minutes.

Yield: 24 squares

	RCU	FU	Cal	%Fat	P	F	C	Na
1 Square	0	0	94	20.8	2	2	18	41

2 Squares = 1 Fruit exchange; 1 1/2 Bread exchange; 1/2 Fat exchange

Chapter Two

Pies

Pies

What could be more appealing than a freshly baked pie or cobbler? Pies have become the specialty and calling-card of many good restaurants. "As American as apple pie" is a saying heard quite often. Memories of childhood often conjure up images of fruit pies cooling on the kitchen windowsill. When one older gentleman was asked, "What is your favorite pie?" he answered, "Hot or cold." His response pretty much sums up how most of us feel about pies.

As you start to make the change to healthier eating, pie doesn't seem to fit in the picture--traditional pie has too much fat and way too much sugar. But if you still yearn for a mouth-watering piece of pie, why not serve a pie that can be healthy, too?

In this chapter you'll find recipes for a variety of pie shells and a variety of pie fillings. The pie crusts range from virtually no-fat varieties all the way to the usual high-fat pie crust. Some will want to serve a pie that contains no sugar but that has a traditional crust. Others will want a low-fat crust as well as a no-sugar filling.

Great pie crusts are tender and flaky--a result of the high fat content. Reduced-fat pie crust recipes will not be as tender and flaky as traditional pie crusts, but they have an excellent taste that accompanies their different texture.

Other recipes include cobblers and crisps. Cobblers are pies that have no bottom crust. Crisps are fruit cobbler fillings with something other than a pie crust on top. They generally have a top crust only or some other type of topping. Any of the pie filling recipes in this chapter can be converted to a cobbler merely by spooning one of the cobbler toppings over the filling.

Especially important when making any pie crust is to roll the pastry on a surface that has been only lightly floured--too much flour tends to toughen the crust. You can further eliminate excess flour by rolling the pastry on a pastry cloth and using a stockinette over the rolling pin. Too much handling of the pastry will also tend to create a tougher crust. When you have the crust rolled out, fold it into quarters and place it gently in the pie pan. Unfold the pastry, being careful not to stretch it; if stretched, the crust will shrink during baking.

For a quick and delicious dessert, make any of the pie or cobbler fillings in this chapter and sprinkle with your homemade granola. If you don't want to make a traditional pie crust, you can still enjoy the bounty of a homemade pie using one of the cobbler toppings. Either one will be a winner with everyone who eats it!

BLUEBERRY COBBLER

This great-tasting cobbler is fun to make during blueberry season.

4	C	fresh or frozen unsweetened blueberries
2	lg	apples, peeled and cut into bite-size pieces
¼	C	sliced almonds, optional
¾	C	unsweetened white grape juice
¼	C	frozen unsweetened apple juice concentrate, thawed
¼	tsp	allspice
1	T	cornstarch
1	C	granola (see recipe chapter 9)

1. Place blueberries, apples, and almonds in 9" x 13" glass baking dish that has been sprayed with nonstick vegetable coating.

2. In a saucepan, combine grape juice, allspice, and cornstarch. Stir until well combined and place over heat, stirring constantly until clear and thick.

3. Pour thickened grape juice over blueberry mixture.

4. Sprinkle granola over top of fruit.

5. Bake at 325° for 30 *35* minutes. *← 6. bake additional 10'*

Yield: 12 servings

	RCU	FU	Cal	%Fat	P	F	C	Na
Per Serving	0	0	103	16	2	2	22	3

1 Serving = 1 Fruit exchange; 1/3 Fat exchange

FRESH PEACH COBBLER

Take advantage of fresh summer peaches to make this delicious dessert. This tastes great whether served warm or cold.

8	med	fresh peaches, sliced
½	C	mashed peach (1 peach)
½	C	water
¼	C	frozen unsweetened apple juice concentrate, thawed
¼	tsp	almond extract
¼	tsp	cinnamon
2	T	cornstarch
½	C	granola (see recipe chapter 9)

1. Slice peaches into a 9" x 9" pan that has been sprayed with nonstick vegetable coating.

2. In a saucepan combine mashed peach, water, apple juice concentrate, almond extract, cinnamon, and cornstarch.

3. Stir constantly over low heat until thickened.

4. Gently fold into sliced peaches.

5. Bake at 350° for 15 minutes.

6. Remove from the oven and sprinkle granola over the top of the peaches; continue to bake for 15 minutes.

Yield: 8 servings

	RCU	FU	Cal	%Fat	P	F	C	Na
Per Serving	0	0	94	11	2	1	21	3

1 Serving = 1 Fruit exchange

CANNED PEACH COBBLER

A year-round version of the famous peach cobbler. Served warm or cold, it will be a family favorite.

1	qt	bottled sliced peaches that have been canned with frozen apple juice concentrate (see recipe chapter 11), drained, saving juice
1	C	peach juice
¼	C	frozen unsweetened apple juice concentrate, thawed
¼	tsp	almond extract
¼	tsp	cinnamon
2	T	cornstarch
½	C	granola (see recipe chapter 9)

1. Drain sliced peaches and save the juice. Combine 1 cup of the peach juice, apple juice concentrate, almond extract, cinnamon, and cornstarch in a saucepan. Stir constantly over low heat until thickened.

2. Place peaches in 9" x 9" pan sprayed with nonstick vegetable coating and pour thickened peach juice mixture over the top.

3. Sprinkle granola over the top of the peach mixture. Bake at 350° for 20 minutes.

Yield: 8 servings

	RCU	FU	Cal	%Fat	P	F	C	Na
Per Serving	0	0	99	3	2	T	24	8

1 Serving = 1 Fruit exchange

RASPBERRY-PEACH COBBLER

A beautiful dessert that will be sure to please all who eat it--a favorite of even the devoted sugar-lover.

1	16-oz. can	unsweetened peach slices, drained, save juice
1	C	unsweetened fresh or frozen raspberries
½	C	peach juice
½	C	frozen unsweetened apple-raspberry juice concentrate, thawed
2	T	cornstarch

1. Drain peaches and measure out 4 oz. of the juice. Combine juice with apple-raspberry concentrate. Stir in cornstarch until well combined.

2. Cook over medium heat, stirring constantly, until thick and clear.

3. When cool, fold in peach slices and raspberries. Divide among four dessert dishes or custard cups. Set aside and make topping.

Topping:

1	T	margarine or butter
2	T	whole wheat flour
4	T	rolled oats
2	T	chopped blanched almonds
¼	tsp	cinnamon
1	T	frozen unsweetened apple juice concentrate, thawed

1. Cut margarine into flour until crumbly. Stir in oats, almonds, and cinnamon.

2. Gently sprinkle in apple juice concentrate until combined.

3. Place in a baking pan and bake at 350° for 10 minutes.

4. Evenly distribute mixture on top of the four dishes.

5. Refrigerate until ready to serve.

Optional topping: For a topping with no added fat, sprinkle with granola instead of using topping recipe.

Yield: 4 servings

	RCU	FU	Cal	%Fat	P	F	C	Na
Per Serving	0	0	205	16	3	4	43	49

1 Serving = 2 Fruit exchange; 1/2 Bread exchange; 1/2 Fat exchange

APPLE-BLACKBERRY COBBLER

An easy and great-tasting fruit dessert.

3 5	C	Rome Beauty (or other red cooking) apples, peeled, cored, and thinly sliced (about 5 large apples)
2 1	C	fresh or frozen blackberries
1½	C	frozen unsweetened apple juice concentrate, thawed
3	T	cornstarch *tapioca*
1	tsp	cinnamon
1 - 2	C	granola (see recipe chapter 9)

1. Combine apple concentrate, cornstarch, and cinnamon; cook over medium heat until mixture comes to a boil; add apple slices and blackberries.

2. Place fruit mixture in a 7" x 11" baking dish. *corningware*

3. Bake at 375° for 25 minutes. *35*

4. Remove from the oven and sprinkle granola evenly over the top; bake for an additional 10 minutes. *covered* *30*

Yield: 10 servings

	RCU	FU	Cal	%Fat	P	F	C	Na
Per Serving	0	0	187	10	2	2	43	12

1 Serving = 2 Fruit exchange; 1/2 Bread exchange

SYLVIA'S TOFU CHERRY COBBLER

Rich in calcium, tofu is a healthy addition to any recipe. This is a tasty and great way to use fresh or frozen sweet cherries.

3	C	pitted fresh or frozen sweet cherries
¾	C	frozen unsweetened apple juice concentrate, thawed
1	C	whole wheat flour
1	tsp	baking powder
4-5	oz	tofu
1	T	cold-pressed oil
½	C	skim milk
¼	C	frozen unsweetened apple juice concentrate, thawed
½	tsp	almond extract

1. Remove pits from 3 cups of cherries; place cherries in a medium saucepan; add 3/4 cup apple concentrate and bring to a boil. Simmer for 5 minutes.

2. Place flour and baking powder in a food processor or blender container; blend together.

3. Add Tofu, oil, milk, 1/4 cup apple juice concentrate, and almond extract to flour mixture; blend until smooth.

4. Spray a 9" x 9" baking pan with nonstick vegetable coating. Spread batter over bottom of prepared pan. Carefully cover with the pitted cherries, then pour the juice over the top of the cherries.

5. Bake at 375° for 40 to 45 minutes.

Yield: 9 servings

	RCU	FU	Cal	%Fat	P	F	C	Na
Per Serving	0	0	187	10	2	2	43	12

1 Serving = 2 Fruit exchange; 1/2 Bread exchange

CHERRY CRISP

A tasty way to use fresh or frozen sweet cherries--and a different twist to the usual toppings.

2	T	cornstarch
⅛	tsp	allspice
2	T	frozen unsweetened apple juice concentrate, thawed
1	C	unsweetened white grape juice
4	C	pitted sweet cherries
½	tsp	almond extract
¾	C	crisp no-sugar brown rice cereal
½	C	whole wheat flour
½	tsp	cinnamon
2	T	frozen unsweetened apple juice concentrate, thawed
2	tsp	margarine or butter, softened

1. Combine cornstarch and allspice in a saucepan; stir in grape juice and apple concentrate until blended. Cook over medium heat, stirring constantly, until clear and thickened. Remove from heat; stir in cherries and almond extract. Pour into 9" x 9" pan sprayed with nonstick vegetable coating.

2. Combine rice cereal, flour, and cinnamon in a bowl. Carefully drizzle apple juice concentrate over the mixture while gently tossing the dry ingredients. Fold softened butter into the mixture until well blended.

3. Evenly distribute the coating over the cherry mixture.

4. Bake at 350° for 25 to 30 minutes.

Yield: 12 servings

	RCU	FU	Cal	%Fat	P	F	C	Na
Per Serving	0	0	92	12	2	1	20	31

1 Serving = 1 Fruit exchange; 1/3 Bread exchange

PEACH AND STRAWBERRY CRISP

You'll look forward to peach season just to be able to make and eat this mouth-watering dessert! With the granola topping, you are looking at no added fat.

6	C	fresh peaches, peeled and sliced (about 3 pounds)
3	C	fresh strawberries, sliced
3	T	cornstarch
1	tsp	cinnamon
1	C	frozen unsweetened apple juice concentrate, thawed
¼	tsp	almond extract
1	C	granola (see recipe chapter 9)

1. Combine first four ingredients in a large bowl, tossing gently to coat. Spoon mixture into a 7" x 11" baking dish that has been sprayed with nonstick vegetable coating.

2. Combine apple juice concentrate and almond extract; pour over the top of the peach and strawberry mixture.

3. Sprinkle the granola evenly over the top of the fruit.

4. Bake at 375° for 25 to 30 minutes, or until bubbly.

Yield: 8 servings

	RCU	FU	Cal	%Fat	P	F	C	Na
Per Serving	0	0	197	11	3	3	44	10

1 Serving = 2 Fruit exchange; 1/2 Bread exchange

STAWBERRY SHORTCAKE

This recipe is lower in fat than the traditional shortcakes, but is still high in fat--so enjoy it only occasionally!

½	C	whole wheat flour
½	C	unbleached white flour
1	tsp	baking powder
3	T	margarine or butter
½	C	skim milk
2	pint	strawberries, washed and hulled
¼	C	frozen unsweetened apple juice concentrate, thawed

1. In medium bowl, combine flours and baking powder; cut in butter with pastry cutter until the butter is crumbly.

2. Stir in 1/2 of the milk; add more gradually until the dough clings together.

3. Drop dough into 6 shortcakes on a cookie sheet that has been sprayed with nonstick vegetable coating. Bake at 400° for 10 to 12 minutes, until light golden brown. Cool.

4. Mash 1/2 of the strawberries; add apple juice concentrate. Slice remainder of the strawberries in quarters and add to strawberry mixture. Serve over shortcake.

Yield: 6 servings

	RCU	FU	Cal	%Fat	P	F	C	Na
Per Serving	0	1	176	31	4	6	28	133

1 Serving = 1 Bread exchange; 1 Fat exchange; 1 Fruit exchange

LOW-FAT PIE CRUST

The usual fat content of a pie crust runs around 65 percent or more. Although the fat content of this crust is lower, you should still eat only a moderate amount.

2	T	margarine or butter
½	C	unbleached flour
½	C	whole wheat flour
6-8	T	ice water

1. Combine whole wheat flour and unbleached flour in a medium bowl.

2. Cut butter into flour with two knives or a pastry blender until crumbly.

3. Add water a tablespoon at a time until dough clings together. Form dough into a flat circle, wrap with plastic wrap, and refrigerate for at least 1/2 hour.

4. Roll out dough on lightly floured surface. For bottom crust only, gently place in 9" pie pan--you can slightly flute edge.

5. For baked pie crust: using table fork, prick bottom and sides of pastry thoroughly. (This keeps shell flat and helps it to hold its shape.) Place in a preheated 425° oven for 10 to 15 minutes or until golden brown. Cool crust and fill as desired.

6. For a two-crust pie: Turn desired filling into a pastry-lined pan. Trim overhanging edge of pastry 1/2" from rim of pan. Roll second round of dough; fold in half. Moisten edges of lower crust with cold water. Transfer top crust to pie pan and roll top edge under lower edge, pinching top and bottom edges together (or press together with fork). Form a stand-up rim on edge of pan to seal well and make fluting easier. Flute edge. To prevent excessive browning, cover edge with a 2" to 3" strip of foil; remove foil during last 15 minutes of baking. Bake pie as directed in individual recipe.

Yield: 1 9" or 10" bottom crust or 1 9" or 10" top crust (10 servings)

	RCU	FU	Cal	%Fat	P	F	C	Na
Per Serving	0	0	61	36	1	2.5	9	27

1 Serving = 1/2 Bread exchange; 1/2 Fat exchange

GRAPE NUTS PIE CRUST

is fair

When you want a pie without all the fat, this is a good recipe to use.

1½ ²	C	Grape Nuts
¾ +	C	frozen unsweetened apple juice concentrate, thawed
½	tsp	vanilla

1. Mix juice concentrate and vanilla with cereal. Let stand until moisture is absorbed.

2. Press into a 9" pie pan.

3. Bake at 350° for 12 minutes.

4. Cool and fill with favorite pie filling.

Yield: 10 servings

	RCU	FU	Cal	%Fat	P	F	C	Na
Per Serving	0	0	96	1	2	T	23	124

1 Serving = 1/2 Fruit exchange; 1/2 Bread exchange

REGULAR PIE CRUST

This recipe is for those who don't want fillings with sugar, but would prefer a regular flaky and tender pie crust. This crust is not low in fat.

2	C	whole wheat flour
2	C	unbleached flour
1½	C	shortening
1	lg	egg white
1	T	vinegar
½	C	cold water

1. Mix flours together; cut in shortening with two knives or a pastry blender until crumbly.

2. In a small bowl, beat together with fork 1/2 cup water, the vinegar, and egg white.

3. Combine the two mixtures, stirring with fork until all ingredients are moistened.

4. Divide dough in 4 portions and shape each portion in a flat round patty ready for rolling.

5. Wrap each in plastic wrap and chill for 1/2 hour.

6. When ready to roll pie crust, lightly flour both sides of patty; put on lightly floured pastry cloth.

7. For bottom crust only, gently place in 9" pie pan--you can flute edge.

8. For baked pie crust: using table fork, prick bottom and sides of pastry thoroughly. (This keeps shell flat and helps it to hold its shape.) Place in preheated 425° oven for 10 to 15 minutes or until golden brown. Cool crust and fill as desired.

9. For a two-crust pie: Turn desired filling into pastry-lined pan. Trim overhanging edge of pastry 1/2" from rim of pan. Roll second round of

dough; fold in half. Moisten edges of lower crust with cold water. Transfer top crust to pie pan and roll top edge under lower edge, pinching top and bottom edges together (or press together with fork). Form a stand-up rim on edge of pan to seal well and make fluting easier. Flute edge. To prevent excessive browning, cover edge with a 2" to 3" strip of foil; remove foil during last 15 minutes of baking. Bake pie as directed in individual recipe.

Yield: 4 single crusts or 40 servings

	RCU	FU	Cal	%Fat	P	F	C	Na
Per Serving	0	1	109	65	2	8	9	2

1 Serving = 1/2 Bread exchange; 1 1/2 Fat exchange

PIE GLAZE

This is a light and shiny glaze similar to pie glazes found in restaurants.

½	C	frozen unsweetened apple-raspberry concentrate, thawed
¼	C	frozen unsweetened apple juice concentrate, thawed
¼	C	water
2	T	cornstarch
6	C	fresh strawberries or sweet cherries

1. Combine juice concentrates and water; whisk cornstarch into cold juice concentrates until dissolved. Heat to boiling over medium heat, stirring constantly.

2. Cool. Gently fold fruit (strawberries or sweet cherries) into glaze. Place in baked 9" pie shell.

Yield: 10 servings

	RCU	FU	Cal	%Fat	P	F	C	Na
Per Serving	0	0	68	5	.7	.4	16	6

1 Serving = 1 Fruit exchange

FRUIT TART

A spectacular looking and tasting dessert. See cover photo.

8–10		fresh strawberries, cut in half
1	sm	kiwifruit
1	sm	banana
		papaya or cantaloupe, slices
		fresh pineapple, cut into triangles

Baked pie shell (not included in recipe breakdown)
Fruit glaze (see recipe below)

1. Bake a pie shell in a tart pan or quiche dish according to pie shell instructions. Let cool.

2. Layer fruit in an attractive pattern. Refer to the front cover for ideas.

3. Cover with fruit glaze by using a pastry brush or carefully spooning the glaze evenly on each piece of fruit.

4. Serve soon after.

Fruit glaze:

1	C	frozen unsweetened apple juice concentrate, thawed
1	T	cornstarch

1. Combine ingredients in a saucepan until smooth; cook, stirring constantly, until thickened.

2. Let cool to room temperature and use as a glaze for the tart.

Yield: 10 servings

	RCU	FU	Cal	%Fat	P	F	C	Na
Per Serving	0	0	74	3	.5	T	18	8

1 Serving = 1 Fruit exchange

Pictured: Cherry Pie, p. 37; Raspberry Peach Cobbler, p. 22; Peach Pie, p. 40; Jumbleberry Pie, p. 38; Crunchy Baked Apples, p. 102.

FRESH STRAWBERRY PIE

Great tasting pie!

6   C   fresh strawberries, washed with stems removed

1 recipe Strawberry Glaze
1 9" baked Grape Nuts Crust

1.   Fill pie crust with strawberries. Pour glaze over the top. Chill and serve.

Strawberry Glaze

This is a full fruit-flavor glaze--it has an excellent taste, but is heavier than glazes seen in restaurants.

1½	C	mashed strawberries
¼	C	frozen unsweetened apple juice concentrate, thawed
¼	C	frozen unsweetened apple-raspberry concentrate, thawed
2	T	cornstarch

1.   Place mashed strawberries into blender container; puree until smooth.

2   In a small saucepan, place pureed strawberries, juice concentrates, and cornstarch; stir until cornstarch is well blended.

3.   Over medium heat, stirring constantly, heat to boiling. Mixture will become thick.

4.   Cool and pour over strawberries in pie crust.

Yield: 10 slices

	RCU	FU	Cal	%Fat	P	F	C	Na
Per Slice	0	0	156	3	3	.6	37	128

1 Slice = 1 1/2 Fruit exchange; 1/2 Bread exchange

Picture: English trifle, p. 56.

FRESH PEACH PIE

A delicious way to use fresh peaches!

6   C   sliced fresh peaches (about 3 pounds)

1 9" baked Grape Nuts Crust
1 recipe Peach Glaze

1.   Place sliced peaches into baked pie crust. Pour Peach Glaze over the top.
     Chill and serve.

Peach Glaze:

1½	C	mashed peaches
½	C	frozen unsweetened apple juice concentrate, thawed
¼	tsp	almond extract
2	T	cornstarch – (not arrowroot!)
		or Tapioca (powdered)

1.   Place mashed peaches into blender container; puree until smooth.

2.   In a small saucepan, place pureed peaches, juice concentrate, almond
     extract, and cornstarch; stir until cornstarch is well blended.

3.   Over medium heat, stirring constantly, heat to boiling. Mixture will
     become a thick and shiny glaze.

4.   Cool and pour over peaches in pie crust.

Yield: 10 slices

	RCU	FU	Cal	%Fat	P	F	C	Na
Per Slice	0	0	193	2	3	.3	47	127

1 Slice = 2 Fruit exchange; 1/2 Bread exchange

APPLE-BLACKBERRY PIE FILLING

A great-tasting pie: the blackberries give it a special twist.

5	C	Rome Beauty (or other red cooking) apples, peeled, cored, and thinly sliced (about 5 large apples)
1	C	fresh or frozen blackberries
1½	C	frozen unsweetened apple juice concentrate, thawed
1	tsp	cinnamon
¼	C	quick-cooking tapioca

1 unbaked 9" two-crust pie shell (not included in recipe breakdown)

1. Combine apple juice concentrate, cinnamon, and tapioca; cook over medium heat until mixture comes to a boil; add apple slices and blackberries and simmer for 15 minutes.

2. Place fruit mixture into a 9" unbaked pie shell; cover with top crust. Brush on egg white mixture (1 large egg white mixed with 2 T water).

3. Bake at 375° for 30 minutes or until lightly browned.

Yield: 10 servings

	RCU	FU	Cal	%Fat	P	F	C	Na
Per Serving	0	0	144	3	.5	.5	36	11

1 Serving = 2 Fruit exchange

APPLE PIE FILLING

This will keep your apple pie traditions alive. Delicious!!!

6	C	Granny Smith apples, peeled, cored, and thinly sliced (about 6 apples)
1½	C	frozen unsweetened apple juice concentrate, thawed
¼	C	quick-cooking tapioca
1	tsp	cinnamon

10-inch two-crust unbaked pie shell (not included in recipe breakdown)

1. Combine juice concentrate, tapioca, and cinnamon; cook over medium heat until mixture comes to a boil. Add apple slices; simmer for 15 minutes. Pour into prepared unbaked pie shell. Cover with top crust.

2. Glaze top crust with egg white mixture (1 egg white mixed with 2 T water).

3. Bake at 375° for 30 minutes, or until lightly browned.

Yield: 10 servings

	RCU	FU	Cal	%Fat	P	F	C	Na
Per Serving	0	0	148	3	.4	.5	37	11

1 Serving = 2 Fruit exchange

CHERRY PIE FILLING

A wonderful tasting pie.

4	C	pitted sweet cherries
1	C	frozen unsweetened apple juice concentrate, thawed
3	T	quick-cooking tapioca
½	tsp	almond extract

1. Place all ingredients in saucepan and cook over medium heat, stirring constantly, until mixture comes to a boil.

2. Place in prepared 9" pie crust and cover with a top crust or a latticed crust as directed in pie crust recipe.

3. Bake at 400° for 10 minutes; lower heat to 350° and bake for an additional 15 minutes, or until crust is a golden brown.

Yield: 10 servings

	RCU	FU	Cal	%Fat	P	F	C	Na
Per Serving	0	0	98	6	1	1	23	8

1 Serving = 1 1/2 Fruit exchange

JUMBLEBERRY PIE FILLING

This deliciously sweet combination of berries makes a wonderful-tasting pie or cobbler.

1	lb	fresh or frozen blueberries
1	lb	fresh or frozen boysenberries
1	lb	fresh or frozen blackberries
½	C	frozen unsweetened grape juice concentrate, thawed
1¼	C	frozen unsweetened apple juice concentrate, thawed
½	C	quick-cooking tapioca
8	oz	unsweetened crushed pineapple, drained

1. Combine juice concentrates, tapioca, and crushed pineapple in a saucepan; cook, stirring constantly, until thickened.

2. Fold berries into thickened juice.

3. Bake as directed for a single crust or double crust pie.

Yield: 1 10-inch pie or 12 servings

	RCU	FU	Cal	%Fat	P	F	C	Na
Per Slice	0	0	159	4	1	.7	39	10

1 Slice = 2 Fruit exchange

BLUEBERRY PIE FILLING

A scrumptious pie. Great in a Grape Nuts crust.

5	C	blueberries (2 lb.)
8	oz can	unsweetened crushed pineapple, undrained
½	C	frozen unsweetened grape juice concentrate, thawed
½	C	frozen unsweetened apple juice concentrate, thawed
¼	C	quick-cooking tapioca

1. Put pineapple, concentrates, and tapioca in a saucepan; bring to a boil, stirring constantly, until thickened.

2. Fold in blueberries. Put in a pie shell, and bake as directed for either a single-crust or a double-crust pie.

3. If you are going to put the filling in an already-baked crust, you will want to add the blueberries to the thickened filling and cook for an additional 3 minutes.

Yield: 1 9- or 10-inch pie, or 10 servings

	RCU	FU	Cal	%Fat	P	F	C	Na
Per Slice	0	0	97	3	1	T	24	9

1 Slice = 1 1/2 Fruit exchange

PEACH PIE FILLING

Great pie during peach season.

3	lb	fresh peaches (about 6 cups sliced)
1	C	frozen unsweetened apple juice concentrate, thawed
¼	C	quick-cooking tapioca
½	tsp	almond extract

1. Combine apple juice concentrate, tapioca, and almond extract in a 4-quart saucepan; soften for 10 minutes. Cook over low heat and bring to a boil; add sliced peaches and cook for an additional 3 minutes.

2. Pour into prepared unbaked 10" pie shell. Cover with a second crust according to the directions of the pie crust recipe.

3. Bake at 375° for 25 to 30 minutes.

Yield: 1 10-inch pie or 12 servings

	RCU	FU	Cal	%Fat	P	F	C	Na
Per Slice	0	0	86	2	1	T	22	6

1 Slice = 1 Fruit exchange

APRICOT PIE FILLING

Take advantage during the short apricot season.

6	C	apricots, cut in half
1	C	frozen unsweetened apple juice concentrate, thawed
¼	C	quick-cooking tapioca
½	tsp	almond extract

1. Combine apple juice concentrate and tapioca in a saucepan. Cook, stirring constantly, until smooth and thick. Remove from heat and stir in almond extract.

2. Fold in apricots.

3. Bake as directed in pie crust recipe.

Yield: 1 9- or 10-inch pie or 10 servings

	RCU	FU	Cal	%Fat	P	F	C	Na
Per Slice	0	0	87	4	1	T	21	7

1 Slice = 1 Fruit exchange

PUMPKIN PIE SQUARES

A very easy version of the all-time-favorite pumpkin pie.

1	lg	apple, peeled and cored
2	lg	eggs
2	lg	egg whites
1	29-oz can	pumpkin
2	tsp	cinnamon
1	tsp	ground ginger
1/2	tsp	ground cloves
1	12-oz can	evaporated skim milk
1	C	frozen unsweetened apple juice concentrate, thawed
1/2	C	skim milk

handwritten note: 2 + syrup
handwritten note: x
handwritten note: A bit tart; could add a little Fruit Sweetner
handwritten note: x

1. Cut apple into thin slices; place on the bottom of a 9 x 13" pan.

2. Place eggs and egg whites into large bowl; beat until blended.

3. Add pumpkin to egg mixture; beat until well blended.

4. Add cinnamon, ground ginger, and ground cloves to pumpkin mixture; beat until well blended.

5. Add evaporated milk, apple juice concentrate, and skim milk; stir until well blended. Pour gently over apple slices.

6. Bake at 350° for 50 to 60 minutes or until a knife inserted into the center comes out clean. Serve cool.

Yield: 12 servings

	RCU	FU	Cal	%Fat	P	F	C	Na
Per Serving	0	0	112	11	4	1	22	66

1 Serving = 1 Fruit exchange; 1/2 Milk exchange; 1/2 Bread exchange

Chapter Three

Cakes

Cakes

Cakes have always been an important part of family traditions. Think about it: whenever you hear the word "cake," you automatically think of birthdays, anniversaries, Christmas fruitcakes, wedding cakes, and those mouth-watering dripper cakes served at family reunions and pot-lucks. There's a good reason for cake's popularity: cakes are fast and easy to make, and everyone enjoys them!

As you improve your eating habits, you don't have to bid farewell to cake. Instead, replace your traditional cake recipes with these low-fat, no-sugar, no-refined-flour versions. These cakes won't be as fluffy, because fluffiness comes from a high fat content. These cakes won't be extremely sweet, either--but you'll love the healthy fruit toppings that will replace your traditional high-sugar frostings.

The recipes in this chapter have been designed for the easiest possible cake: simply leave the cake in the pan and cover it with one of the listed fruit toppings. If you want to, you can easily bake any of these cakes in two 8" or 9" round cake pans instead of in the listed 9" x 13" pan. When baking a cake that you will remove from the pan, line the bottom of your pan with waxed paper--you'll be able to easily remove the cake without breaking or crumbling it. If you make a two-layer cake, put fruit topping between and on top of the layers.

FRUITCAKE

You will never miss the sugar or fat in this delicious fruitcake. This was one of the most popular and requested recipes by all those who ate it. Use this recipe to keep your Christmas traditions alive, but be sure to freeze extra bags of cranberries so this recipe may be served at times other than during the Christmas holidays.

¼	C	frozen unsweetened apple juice concentrate, thawed
¾	C	frozen unsweetened orange juice concentrate, thawed
1	C	cranberries, chopped
1½	C	pitted dates, chopped
1	C	pecans, chopped
1	tsp	grated orange rind
1	tsp	vanilla
2	lg	egg whites
1	8-oz. can	unsweetened pineapple tidbits, drained
1¾	C	whole wheat flour
1¼	tsp	baking soda
½	tsp	cinnamon
¼	tsp	nutmeg
¼	tsp	allspice

1. Combine apple juice, orange juice, and cranberries in a large bowl; cover and let stand 45 minutes.

2. Combine dates, pecans, orange rind, vanilla, egg whites, and pineapple. Add to cranberry mixture; stir well.

3. Combine dry ingredients; add to fruit mixture and stir well.

4. Pour batter into 6-cup Bundt pan coated with nonstick vegetable spray.

5. Bake at 325° for 40 minutes or until a wooden pick inserted in cake comes out clean. Cool cake in pan 20 minutes; remove from pan, and let cool on a wire rack.

6. Cover cake with plastic wrap, and then aluminum foil. Store in a cool place for several days before serving.

Yield: 16 servings

	RCU	FU	Cal	%Fat	P	F	C	Na
Per serving	0	.5	179	25	3	5	33	73

1 Serving = 1 Fruit exchange; 1/2 Bread exchange; 1 Fat exchange

APPLE CAKE

Of Norwegian origin, this cake looks more like a pie. The sliced almonds in a flower shape on top add an attractive touch.

¾	C	whole wheat flour
½	tsp	baking powder
½	tsp	baking soda
1	tsp	cinnamon
2	lg	cooking apples, unpeeled, cored, and chopped
1	lg	egg white
1	tsp	vanilla
½	C	frozen unsweetened apple juice concentrate, thawed
¼	C	chopped almonds

sliced almonds

1. Combine flour, baking powder, baking soda, and cinnamon in a mixing bowl; mix well.

2. Add apples, stirring lightly to coat. Add egg white, vanilla, and juice concentrate to apple mixture; stir until well blended.

3. Spoon mixture into a 9-inch pie plate sprayed with nonstick vegetable coating. Sprinkle chopped almonds around the edge of the pie plate. Arrange sliced almonds into a flower shape in the center of the pan, if desired.

4. Bake at 350° (325° if using a glass pie plate) for 30 to 35 minutes, or until lightly browned.

Yield: 6 to 8 servings

	RCU	FU	Cal	%Fat	P	F	C	Na
Per Serving	0	0	128	20	3	3	24	83

1 Serving = 1 Fruit exchange; 1/2 Bread exchange; 1/2 Fat exchange

APPLESAUCE CAKE

A delicious cake by itself or with the apple topping.

¼	C	cold-pressed oil
1½	C	frozen unsweetened apple juice concentrate, thawed
3	lg	egg whites
½	C	unsweetened applesauce
1	tsp	vanilla
2½	C	whole wheat flour
1	C	quick-cooking rolled oats
¾	tsp	baking soda
2	tsp	baking powder
1	tsp	cinnamon
½	tsp	nutmeg
½	C	raisins
1	C	grated apple, peeled and cored (1 large apple)

1. Preheat oven to 375°. Spray 9" x 13" cake pan with nonstick vegetable coating. If you are going to remove the cake whole from the pan, line the bottom of the pan with waxed paper.

2. Beat together oil, apple concentrate, and egg whites. Add applesauce and vanilla; combine well.

3. Mix together flour, oats, soda, baking powder, cinnamon, and nutmeg; add to the liquid mixture and beat. Add raisins and grated apple; stir until blended.

4. Pour batter into prepared pan. Bake for 25 to 30 minutes or until a wooden pick inserted in the center comes out clean.

Yield: 24 servings

	RCU	FU	Cal	%Fat	P	F	C	Na
Per Serving	0	0	121	19	3	3	22	60

1 Serving= 3/4 Fruit exchange; 3/4 Bread exchange; 1/2 Fat exchange

CHRISTMAS FRUITCAKE

A delicious variation of famous high-calorie fruitcakes. Your friends and family will love receiving this for a gift!

¾	C	dried apricots
¾	C	frozen unsweetened orange juice, thawed
1	C	dried apples, chopped
1	C	dried figs, chopped
1	C	frozen unsweetened apple juice concentrate, thawed
2	C	currants
2	C	walnuts, chopped
2	C	whole wheat flour
1	tsp	cinnamon
1	tsp	nutmeg
1	tsp	allspice
¼	tsp	ground cloves
1	tsp	baking powder
½	tsp	baking soda
3	lg	egg whites
¼	C	cold-pressed oil
1	tsp	grated orange peel
1	tsp	vanilla

additional frozen apple juice concentrate, thawed

1. Spray two 8" x 4" loaf pans with nonstick vegetable coating; line bottom of pans with brown paper.

2. Place apricots and orange juice in a small saucepan. Bring to a boil, then cover pan and turn off heat. Let sit for 5 minutes. Meanwhile, chop figs and apples.

3. Drain apricots, reserving juice in a 1-cup measuring cup. Put figs and apples in saucepan with the 1 cup apple juice concentrate; bring to a boil, then cover pan and turn off heat.

4. Let sit for 5 minutes, then drain, adding any extra liquid to the 1-cup measure. Meanwhile, chop the apricots.

5. Combine chopped apricots, figs, apples, currants, and nuts in a large mixing bowl. Preheat oven to 300°.

6. Combine flour with spices, baking powder, and soda.

7. Combine egg whites, oil, orange peel, and vanilla. Add more apple juice concentrate to the reserved fruit juice in the 1-cup measure, up to the 1-cup mark, and add to eggs.

8. Stir flour mixture into egg mixture, then stir batter into dried fruits and nuts.

9. Pour batter into the two loaf pans and bake for about 45 to 60 minutes. Test by inserting a wooden pick. It will come out clean when fruitcakes are done.

10. Let cakes cool in pans on racks until they reach room temperature, then remove. Wrap the cakes in aluminum foil.

Yield: 2 fruit cakes or 32 servings

	RCU	FU	Cal	%Fat	P	F	C	Na
Per Serving	0	0	115	16	2	2	24	34

1 Slice = 1 Fruit exchange; 1/3 Bread exchange; 1/3 Fat exchange

STRAWBERRY CHEESECAKE

This is a tasty version of the famous high-fat cheesecake.

2	C	fresh strawberries
2	med	bananas, sliced
2	C	Ricotta cheese (15-oz carton)
1	tsp	vanilla
2	lg	egg whites
2	env	unflavored gelatin
½	C	frozen unsweetened apple juice concentrate, thawed

1 unbaked Grape Nuts pie shell (see recipe below)

1. Wash, hull, and crush enough strawberries (about 15) to measure 1 cup. Slice bananas.

2. Warm apple juice concentrate slightly and sprinkle gelatin on top; stir and let stand until gelatin is dissolved.

3. Place strawberries and bananas into blender container; blend until smooth. Add vanilla and slowly add Ricotta cheese; blend well.

4. Add gelatin mixture and egg whites; blend well.

5. Pour into unbaked Grape Nuts crust. Bake at 350° for 1 hour. Remove from oven and cool.

6. Refrigerate for 3 hours; serve. Garnish with remaining strawberries.

Crust:

1	C	Grape Nuts
⅓	C	frozen unsweetened apple juice concentrate, thawed
¼	tsp	vanilla

1. Mix all ingredients in a bowl. Let stand a few minutes until liquid is absorbed. Press into a 9" round cake pan or spring-form pan to cover bottom of pan.

To serve: Take 1 pint strawberries, washed and hulled, slightly mash with 2 Tbsp apple juice concentrate and drizzle over each slice.

Yield: 10 servings

	RCU	FU	Cal	%Fat	P	F	C	Na
Per Slice	0	0	195	19.7	10	4	31	158

1 Slice = 1 1/2 Fruit exchange; 1/2 Bread exchange

POOR MAN'S CAKE

This moist and delicious cake doesn't use eggs and needs no frosting. Great for picnics.

2	C	raisins
¼	C	margarine or butter
1½	C	frozen unsweetened apple juice concentrate, thawed
1½	C	water
2	tsp	nutmeg
2	tsp	cinnamon
½	tsp	cloves
1	T	cocoa
2	tsp	soda
3½	C	whole wheat flour

1. Boil together in saucepan the raisins, margarine, apple juice concentrate, water, nutmeg, cinnamon, cloves, and cocoa; cool.

2. When cool, add soda; stir. Add flour to make batter not too thin or too stiff. Pour batter into 9" x 13" pan that has been sprayed with nonstick vegetable coating.

3. Bake at 300° for 40 to 45 minutes, or until a wooden pick inserted into the center comes out clean.

Yield: 24 servings

	RCU	FU	Cal	%Fat	P	F	C	Na
Per Serving	0	0	143	16	3	3	30	95

1 Serving = 1 Fruit exchange; 1 Bread exchange

APPLE PRUNE CAKE

This cake is an immediate favorite--but no one knows that it has prunes in it. (Most guess that its sweetness comes from dates). Good with apple topping.

⅓	C	cold-pressed oil
3	lg	egg whites
1½	C	frozen unsweetened apple juice concentrate, thawed
½	C	unsweetened applesauce
3½	C	whole wheat flour
2	tsp	baking powder
1	tsp	baking soda
1	tsp	cinnamon
½	tsp	nutmeg
1-2	C	apples, peeled and finely diced
1-1½	C	prunes, pitted and finely chopped
½-1	C	walnuts, chopped, optional

1. Cream oil and egg whites until fluffy.

2. Beat in apple juice concentrate and applesauce until smooth.

3. Add flour, baking powder, baking soda, cinnamon, and nutmeg; beat until smooth.

4. Fold in apples, prunes, and walnuts.

5. Spoon into a 9" x 13" pan that has been sprayed with nonstick vegetable coating.

6. Bake at 350° for 30̶ 35 minutes. *uncovered + 30' covered*

Yield: 24 servings

	RCU	FU	Cal	%Fat	P	F	C	Na
Per Serving	0	0	119	5	3	1	27	72

1 Serving = 1 Fruit exchange; 1 Bread exchange

BOILED RAISIN CAKE

A very tasty cake that will delight raisin lovers.

2	C	raisins
2	C	frozen unsweetened apple juice concentrate, thawed
3½	C	whole wheat flour
2	tsp	baking soda
2	tsp	cinnamon
1½	tsp	nutmeg
½	tsp	ground cloves
⅓	C	margarine or butter, melted
3	lg	egg whites
2	tsp	vanilla
1½	tsp	mapeline
½	C	walnuts, chopped, optional

1. Boil raisins in apple juice concentrate for 10 minutes; reserve liquid and add enough water to make 2 cups liquid. Set aside.

2. In large bowl combine flour, baking soda, cinnamon, nutmeg, and cloves. Add melted butter, egg whites, vanilla, mapeline, and liquid from raisins; blend thoroughly.

3. Fold in raisins and nuts.

4. Pour into 9" x 13" pan that has been sprayed with nonstick vegetable coating. Bake at 350° for 30 to 35 minutes or until a wooden pick inserted in center comes out clean.

Yield: 24 servings

	RCU	FU	Cal	%Fat	P	F	C	Na
Per Serving	0	0	160	17	3	3	32	112

1 Serving = 1 Fruit exchange; 1 Bread exchange; 1/2 Fat exchange

DATE CAKE

This is a winner when it comes to taste. It needs no extra topping--it's rich enough without it.

3	lg	egg whites
3	T	cold-pressed oil
1	tsp	vanilla
½	C	frozen unsweetened apple juice concentrate, thawed
½	C	unsweetened applesauce
½	C	banana, mashed
1	C	dates, chopped
2	C	whole wheat flour
⅓	C	wheat germ
2	tsp	baking powder
1	tsp	baking soda

1. Preheat oven to 350°. Spray a 9" x 9" baking pan with nonstick vegetable coating.

2. Combine egg whites and oil; beat well. Add vanilla, apple juice concentrate, applesauce, and bananas; mix well.

3. Coat chopped dates in flour.

4. Combine flour-date mixture, wheat germ, baking powder, and baking soda. Add to the liquid mixture. Mix well.

5. Pour into prepared pan. Bake for 25 to 30 minutes or until a wooden pick inserted into the center comes out clean.

Optional Topping:

Sprinkle chopped walnuts and additional chopped date pieces on top of the batter before it is baked. Bake as directed.

Yield: 16 servings

	RCU	FU	Cal	%Fat	P	F	C	Na
Per Serving	0	0	143	20	4	3	27	103

1 Serving = 1 Fruit exchange; 1 Bread exchange; 1/2 Fat exchange

BANANA-STRAWBERRY CAKE

Great to eat as is or to use in an English Trifle. Can be frosted with the strawberry topping.

½	C	fresh strawberries, crushed
1	C	bananas, mashed
¼	C	cold-pressed oil
3	lg	egg whites
1½	C	frozen unsweetened apple juice concentrate, thawed
2½	C	whole wheat flour
1½	C	quick-cooking rolled oats
1	tsp	baking soda
2	tsp	baking powder

1. Preheat oven to 350°. Spray 9" x 13" pan with nonstick vegetable coating.

2. Combine egg whites and oil; beat well. Add strawberries, bananas, and apple juice concentrate; beat well.

3. Combine flour, oats, baking soda, and baking powder; add to the liquid mixture and beat well.

4. Pour into prepared pan and bake for 25 minutes or until a wooden pick inserted into the center comes out clean.

Yield: 24 servings

	RCU	FU	Cal	%Fat	P	F	C	Na
Per Serving	0	0	126	21	3	3	23	72

1 Serving = 1/2 Fruit exchange; 1 Bread exchange; 1/2 Fat exchange

ENGLISH TRIFLE

This is a very elegant and impressive-looking dessert geared for a large crowd. Make it part of your favorite dinner-party menu.

Make the Banana Strawberry cake (see recipe), pouring the batter into two 8" round cake pans. Bake for 30 to 35 minutes.

Remove from pans and let cool. Line clean 8" round cake pans with plastic wrap, and place cooled cake back in pan.

Make gelatin:

1	env	unflavored gelatin
¼	C	water
¾	C	water
⅔	C	frozen unsweetened apple-raspberry concentrate, thawed

1. Soften gelatin in 1/4 cup water for 5 minutes. Bring 3/4 cup water to a boil. Pour over softened gelatin.

2. When gelatin is dissolved, add juice concentrate and stir until well blended. Set aside to cool.

3. Poke holes in the tops of cakes. Pour room-temperature gelatin evenly over the tops of cooled cakes; refrigerate to set.

Make Banana Pudding (see recipe in Pudding chapter).

To assemble:

1. Place one layer of the cake in trifle bowl (trim if needed to make it fit). Top with one half of the banana pudding. Layer drained 8 oz. can of pineapple tidbits over top of pudding. Around the edges, place strawberry halves (cut lengthwise) around the edges with triangles of kiwi fruit between the strawberries.

2. Place second layer of cake over fruit and pudding. Spread remaining pudding over the top. Decorate with strawberry halves and triangles of

kiwi fruit around the edges. Garnish with additional round slices of kiwi fruit and raspberries.

Yield: 24 servings

	RCU	FU	Cal	%Fat	P	F	C	Na
Per Serving	0	0	175	16	4	3	35	73

1 Serving = 1 1/2 Fruit exchange; 1 Bread exchange; 1/2 Fat exchange

BANANA CAKE

Banana cakes are always a winner. Top with the strawberry topping for a different taste.

⅓	C	cold-pressed oil
3	lg	egg whites
1	C	mashed bananas
1	C	frozen unsweetened apple juice concentrate, thawed
2¼	C	whole wheat flour
2	tsp	baking powder
1	tsp	baking soda
1½	tsp	cinnamon
½	C	walnuts, chopped (optional)

1. Preheat oven to 350°. Spray a 9" x 9" baking pan with nonstick vegetable coating.

2. Combine egg whites and oil; beat well. Add mashed bananas and apple juice concentrate; beat well.

3. Combine flour, baking powder, baking soda, and cinnamon; add to the liquid mixture. Mix well.

4. Stir in nuts.

5. Bake at 350° for about 30 minutes or until a wooden pick inserted into the center comes out clean.

Yield: 16 servings.

	RCU	FU	Cal	%Fat	P	F	C	Na
Per Serving	0	0	129	21	3	3	24	105

1 Serving = 3/4 Fruit exchange; 3/4 Bread exchange; 1/2 Fat exchange

PUMPKIN APPLE CAKE

This delicious cake is a good way to use pumpkin!

⅓	C	cold-pressed oil
2	lg	egg whites
1	C	canned pumpkin
1½	C	frozen unsweetened apple juice concentrate, thawed
1	tsp	vanilla
½	C	unsweetened applesauce
3	C	whole wheat flour
1	tsp	cinnamon
2	tsp	baking powder
1	tsp	baking soda
⅓	C	pecans, chopped
1	C	apple, peeled and finely diced

1. Cream oil and egg whites until fluffy.

2. Beat in pumpkin, apple juice concentrate, vanilla, and applesauce.

3. Add flour, cinnamon, baking powder, and baking soda.

4. Fold in pecans and diced apple.

5. Spoon batter into a 9" x 13" pan sprayed with nonstick vegetable coating.

6. Bake at 350° for 35 minutes.

Yield: 24 Servings

	RCU	FU	Cal	%Fat	P	F	C	Na
Per Serving	0	0	112	22	3	3	21	70

1 Serving = 1/2 Fruit exchange; 3/4 Bread exchange; 1/2 Fat exchange

PINEAPPLE CAKE

The pineapple topping makes this cake attractive--and great-tasting, too!

4	lg	egg whites
3	T	cold-pressed oil
½	tsp	vanilla
½	tsp	almond extract
¼	C	frozen unsweetened pineapple juice concentrate, thawed
½	C	frozen unsweetened apple juice concentrate, thawed
½	C	unsweetened applesauce or mashed banana
¾	C	unsweetened crushed pineapple
2	C	whole wheat flour
¼	C	oat bran
1	tsp	baking soda
½	tsp	cinnamon

1. Preheat oven to 350°. Spray 9" x 9" baking pan with nonstick vegetable coating. Line with waxed paper if you are going to remove the cake whole.

2. Combine egg whites and oil and beat well. Add vanilla, almond extract, pineapple concentrate, applesauce or banana, and crushed pineapple; mix well.

3. Combine flour, oat bran, baking soda, and cinnamon. Add to the liquid mixture, blending well.

4. Pour batter into prepared pan. Bake at 350° for 25 to 30 minutes or until browned. Cool and top with pineapple topping.

Yield: 12 servings

	RCU	FU	Cal	%Fat	P	F	C	Na
Per Serving	0	0	152	24	4	4	26	89

1 Serving = 1/2 Fruit exchange; 1 Bread exchange; 1/2 Fat exchange

PINEAPPLE TOPPING

You'll love this easy-to-make cake topping.

¾	C	crushed pineapple with juice
2	T	frozen unsweetened apple juice concentrate, thawed
1	T	cornstarch
½	tsp	coconut extract

1. Place crushed pineapple in a saucepan. With the heat off, stir in the cornstarch until well blended.

2. Add the pineapple concentrate and coconut extract. Cook over low-medium heat, stirring constantly until clear and thickened.

3. Cool and spread over pineapple cake.

Yield: Topping for a 9" x 13" cake (24 servings)

	RCU	FU	Cal	%Fat	P	F	C	Na
Per Serving	0	0	17	1	0	0	4	1

1 Serving = 1/4 Fruit exchange

APPLE TOPPING

Great tasting apple topping.

1	T	margarine or butter
3	C	apples, peeled, cored, and sliced 1/4-inch thick
½	tsp	cinnamon
½	C	frozen unsweetened apple juice concentrate, thawed

1. Melt margarine in skillet over moderate heat. Add apples and apple juice concentrate; sprinkle cinnamon over top of apples.

2. Cook until apples are tender and syrupy. Cool.

3. Remove apples only and place them on top of the cake in a neat pattern. Gently spoon syrup over the top of the apples, evenly distributing it over the top of the cake.

Yield: Topping for a 9" x 13" cake (24 servings)

	RCU	FU	Cal	%Fat	P	F	C	Na
Per Serving	0	0	21	16.7	T	.4	5	5

1 Serving = 1/4 Fruit serving

STRAWBERRY TOPPING

Great tasting strawberry topping.

¼	C	frozen unsweetened apple-raspberry concentrate, thawed
2	T	frozen unsweetened apple juice concentrate, thawed
2	T	water
1	T	cornstarch
2	C	sliced fresh strawberries

1. Combine juice concentrates and water; whisk cornstarch into cold juice concentrates until dissolved. Heat to boiling over medium heat, stirring constantly.

2. Cool. Gently fold strawberries into glaze. Distribute evenly over the top of cake.

Yield: Topping for a 9" x 13" cake (24 servings)

	RCU	FU	Cal	%Fat	P	F	C	Na
Per Serving	0	0	12	5	T	T	3	1

1 Serving = 1/4 Fruit exchange

Chapter Four

Gelatin

Gelatins

Gelatin desserts have been advertised for years as the perfect ending to any meal. Why? Because there's always room for gelatin! Gelatin provides a light finish after eating--something sweet but not too heavy. Unfortunately, the picture's not completely perfect: all available gelatins are primarily either sugar or artificial sweeteners, neither one a very good choice.

With the recipes in this chapter, you now have a choice! The salads or desserts in this chapter are sweet and delicious, and the people you serve them to will probably think they came out of a box. There's really only one limitation: these natural fruit gelatins don't come in a rainbow of colors, since there is no sweet alternative to green or yellow.

Serve one of these scrumptious desserts at your next dinner, then sit back and listen to the compliments. If you haven't served a gelatin for awhile because you've been cutting back on sugar, you may just pleasantly astound your family!

Pictured: Boysenberry Gelatin, p. 68; Waldorf Gelatin, p. 74; Orange Gelatin, p. 71; Raspberry Pineapple Gelatin with bananas, p. 66; Spring Fruit Gelatin, p. 67; White Grape Juice Gelatin, p. 70.

JOLAYNE'S STRAWBERRY MOUSSE

This is a great-tasting and beautiful dessert. Your guests will love it.

1	C	frozen unsweetened apple juice concentrate, thawed
1½	env	plain gelatin
1	C	pureed strawberries
1	C	plain nonfat yogurt
2	C	sliced strawberries

1. Soften gelatin in apple juice concentrate for 5 minutes. Bring to a boil, stirring constantly, until gelatin is dissolved.

2. Add pureed strawberries to gelatin; mix well. Refrigerate until the mixture is the consistency of egg whites.

3. Remove from refrigerator and add yogurt. With electric mixer, whip until light and frothy.

4. Fold in sliced strawberries and pour into serving bowl or individual dessert dishes.

5. Refrigerate until firm.

Yield: 10 Servings

	RCU	FU	Cal	%Fat	P	F	C	Na
Per Serving	0	0	81	4	2.8	3.7	18	26

1 Serving = 1 Fruit exchange

Pictured: Pineapple Cake with Pineapple Topping, p. 60, 61; Strawberry Sorbet, p. 94; Frozen Blueberry Yogurt, p. 89; Applesauce Cake with Apple Topping, p. 47, 61.

RASPBERRY-PINEAPPLE GELATIN

This is a delicious gelatin dessert that can also be served as a salad on a lettuce leaf. No one will miss the sugar.

1	C	water
2	env	unflavored gelatin
1	12-oz can	frozen unsweetened apple-raspberry juice concentrate
½	C	unsweetened pineapple juice
1	T	lemon juice
1	C	fresh or frozen unsweetened raspberries
1	C	unsweetened crushed pineapple, drained

1. Measure water into a pan and pour in gelatin. Let the gelatin soften for about 5 minutes. Bring to a boil, stirring constantly, until gelatin is dissolved.

2. Add the juice concentrate, pineapple juice, and lemon juice.

3. Stir in fruit, and pour into a 1 1/2-quart bowl or into individual serving dishes for dessert. You can also pour the gelatin into a square pan and serve squares of the gelatin on lettuce leaves for a salad. Refrigerate until firm.

Yield: 9 square salad servings or 6 dessert servings

	RCU	FU	Cal	%Fat	P	F	C	Na
Per Serving	0	0	116	2	2	T	27	14

1 Serving = 2 Fruit exchanges

SPRING FRUIT GELATIN

Pineapple, strawberries, and bananas are a sure winner in this fruit gelatin.

1	8-oz can	unsweetened pineapple tidbits
1¼	C	water
2	env	plain unflavored gelatin
1	12-oz can	frozen unsweetened Fruit 'n Berry or Apple-Raspberry concentrate
1	tsp	lemon juice
1	C	plain nonfat yogurt
1	C	sliced fresh strawberries
1	C	sliced bananas

1. Drain pineapple tidbits, reserving juice.

2. In small saucepan, soften gelatin in 1 1/4 cups water; let sit for 5 minutes. Bring mixture to a boil to dissolve gelatin.

3. Add concentrate, reserved pineapple juice, and lemon juice to dissolved gelatin. Chill gelatin mixture until slightly thickened. Whip gelatin until fluffy.

4. Beat in yogurt until well blended.

5. Fold in pineapple, strawberries, and bananas.

6. Spoon mixture into 7-cup gelatin mold. Chill until firm.

7. Unmold onto serving plate.

Yield: 12 (1/2-cup) servings

	RCU	FU	Cal	%Fat	P	F	C	Na
Per Serving	0	0	113	3	3	.4	26	25

1 Serving = 1 1/2 Fruit exchange

BOYSENBERRY GELATIN

This delicious boysenberry-flavored dessert can also be served as a salad.

2	env	plain unflavored gelatin
3	C	unsweetened Boysenberry juice
1	T	lemon juice
1½	C	unsweetened frozen or fresh boysenberries
1	8-oz can	unsweetened crushed pineapple, drained

1. In a small saucepan dissolve gelatin in one cup of the boysenberry juice; let stand 5 minutes to soften.

2. Stir over low heat until gelatin is completely dissolved.

3. Combine gelatin mixture, boysenberry juice, lemon juice, and fruit in a 1 1/2-quart dessert bowl or individual dessert bowls.

4. Chill until firm.

Yield: 8 (1/2-cup) servings

	RCU	FU	Cal	%Fat	P	F	C	Na
Per Serving	0	0	81	2	2.4	.2	18	9

1 Serving = 1 Fruit exchange

SPARKLING BERRY GELATIN

A very pretty dessert that tastes good, too.

2	env	plain unflavored gelatin
1	12-oz can	frozen unsweetened apple-raspberry concentrate, thawed
½	C	water
1	C	club soda
1	tsp	lemon juice
3	C	assorted blueberries, raspberries, and strawberries

1. Combine juice concentrate and water.

2. In small saucepan, sprinkle gelatin over 1 cup of the juice. Let stand 5 minutes. Stir over low heat until gelatin is completely dissolved.

3. In large bowl, blend remaining 1 cup juice, soda, gelatin mixture, and lemon juice. Chill, stirring occasionally, until mixture is the consistency of unbeaten egg whites, about 60 minutes.

4. Fold in berries. Pour into individual serving dishes.

5. Chill until firm, about 3 hours.

Yield: 12 (1/2-cup) servings

	RCU	FU	Cal	%Fat	P	F	C	Na
Per Serving	0	0	79	3.6	1.6	.3	18	15

1 Serving = 1 Fruit exchange

WHITE GRAPE JUICE GELATIN

This attractive gelatin dessert tastes great, too!

2	env	unflavored gelatin
½	C	cold water
3	C	unsweetened white grape juice
2	C	green grapes

1. Soften gelatin in water and let sit for 5 minutes.

2. Bring grape juice to a boil; stir into softened gelatin. Stir until dissolved.

3. Refrigerate mixture until it reaches the consistency of egg whites. Stir in grapes. Pour into dessert dishes or goblets.

4. Refrigerate until firm.

Yield: 6 servings

	RCU	FU	Cal	%Fat	P	F	C	Na
Per Serving	0	0	106	1.8	3	T	24	7

1 Serving = 1 1/2 Fruit exchanges

ORANGE GELATIN

Refreshing gelatin dessert.

1	C	water
2	env	unflavored gelatin
¾	C	frozen unsweetened pineapple-orange juice concentrate, thawed
¾	C	water
1	T	lemon juice
1	15-oz can	unsweetened crushed pineapple, undrained
1	11-oz can	unsweetened mandarin oranges, drained

1. Soften gelatin in 1 cup water; let sit for 5 minutes.

2. Bring juice concentrate and 3/4 cup water to a boil; stir into softened gelatin. Stir until dissolved.

3. Add lemon juice and crushed pineapple. Refrigerate mixture until it reaches the consistency of egg whites.

4. Fold in drained mandarin oranges. Spoon mixture into dessert dishes or goblets.

Yield: 6 servings

	RCU	FU	Cal	%Fat	P	F	C	Na
Per Serving	0	0	124	.7	5	T	28	8

1 Serving = 1 1/2 Fruit exchange

GRAPE GELATIN

Quick and easy light gelatin dessert.

2	env	unflavored gelatin
½	C	cold water
3	C	unsweetened grape juice
2	C	sliced banana

1. Soften gelatin in water and let sit for 5 minutes.

2. Bring grape juice to a boil; stir into softened gelatin. Stir until dissolved.

3. Refrigerate mixture until it reaches the consistency of egg whites. Spoon mixture into a 6-cup mold and chill until firm.

Yield: 6 servings

	RCU	FU	Cal	%Fat	P	F	C	Na
Per Serving	0	0	157	3	4	.5	37	7

1 Serving = 2 Fruit exchange

FRUIT JUICE SQUARES

This is a wonderful no-sugar version of the famous Knox Blox that are so popular with children everywhere.

1	12-oz	frozen unsweetened Fruit and Berry concentrate (or
	can	any other 12 oz. unsweetened fruit juice), thawed
2½	C	water
4	env	unflavored gelatin

1. Dissolve the juice concentrate in the water.

2. Measure out 1 cup of the juice and sprinkle the 4 packages of unflavored gelatin over it. Let this soften about 5 minutes.

3. Bring the remaining juice to a boil and pour into the gelatin mixture. Stir until dissolved.

4. Pour into a 9" x 13" pan. Refrigerate until firm. Cut into 1" squares.

Yield: 9 dozen 1" squares

	RCU	FU	Cal	%Fat	P	F	C	Na
Per Serving	0	0	8	2	T	0	2	1

5 Squares = 1/2 Fruit exchange

WALDORF GELATIN SALAD

A delicious version of the famous Waldorf salad--without the sugar and the fat.

2	env	unflavored gelatin
1½	C	water
1	T	lemon juice
1	12-oz	frozen unsweetened apple-cranberry concentrate,thawed
½	C	chopped walnuts, optional
1	lg	red apple, chopped (do not peel)
½	C	celery, chopped fine

1. Soften gelatin in water and let sit for 5 minutes. Bring to a boil until gelatin is dissolved.

2. Add lemon juice and frozen concentrate.

3. Add walnuts, apple, and celery; stir gently. Pour into an 8" x 8" glass dish. Refrigerate until firm.

4. Serve on a lettuce leaf.

Yield: 9 servings

	RCU	FU	Cal	%Fat	P	F	C	Na
Per Serving	0	0	98	2	2	.2	23	19

1 Serving = 1 1/2 Fruit exchange

CRANBERRY GELATIN SALAD

A delicious gelatin salad that is wonderful with any holiday meal. Freeze an extra bag of cranberries so that you can enjoy this during other times of the year.

2	env	unflavored gelatin
1½	C	water
1	T	lemon juice
1	12-oz can	frozen unsweetened apple-cranberry concentrate
½	C	cranberries, chopped
¾	C	red apple, chopped (do not peel)
½	C	celery, chopped fine
½	C	halved seedless green grapes
¼	C	chopped walnuts, optional

1. Soften gelatin in water and let sit for 5 minutes. Bring to a boil until gelatin is dissolved.

2. Add lemon juice and frozen juice concentrate.

3. Add the remainder of the ingredients and stir gently. Pour into an 8" x 8" glass dish. Refrigerate until firm.

4. Serve on a lettuce leaf.

Yield: 9 servings

	RCU	FU	Cal	%Fat	P	F	C	Na
Per Serving	0	0	107	3	2	.3	25	20

1 Serving = 1 1/2 Fruit exchange

SUNSHINE SALAD

A colorful gelatin salad that will make a nice accompaniment to any meal. Serve on a lettuce leaf.

1	C	water
3	env	unflavored gelatin
¾	C	frozen unsweetened pineapple-orange juice concentrate, thawed
¾	C	water
1	T	lemon juice
1	15-oz can	unsweetened crushed pineapple, undrained
1	C	grated carrots

1. Soften gelatin in 1 cup water; let sit for 5 minutes.

2. Bring juice concentrate and 3/4 cup water to a boil; stir into gelatin until dissolved.

3. Add lemon juice, pineapple, and carrots.

4. Pour into an 11" x 7" pan and refrigerate until firm.

Yield: 10 Servings

	RCU	FU	Cal	%Fat	P	F	C	Na
Per Serving	0	0	78	1	2.8	T	18	8

1 Serving = 1 Fruit exchange

Chapter Five

Pudding

Puddings

Puddings were one of the most difficult desserts to convert. There are several reasons why. First, there is a tendency for the fruit juices to curdle the milk if you aren't careful. And, of course, high-fat egg yolks are generally one of the thickening agents used in puddings--and to keep the fat content of these puddings down, something else had to be used.

The following recipes are pleasant alternatives to eliminating pudding. You'll love the variety that's included. Bread puddings have been a long-time tradition in many families--and in Southern restaurants, bread pudding is a specialty. Tapioca is always creamy, cool, and refreshing. And the pumpkin pudding is a nice alternative to pumpkin pie--without a high-fat crust to deal with!

PINEAPPLE PUDDING

A light refreshing dessert.

¾	C	unsweetened canned pineapple juice
1	env	unflavored gelatin
1½	C	unsweetened crushed pineapple, well drained
¼	C	frozen unsweetened apple juice concentrate, thawed
1½	C	plain nonfat yogurt

1. Pour 1/2 cup pineapple juice into a small saucepan, and sprinkle gtelatin on top. Let stand for about 5 minutes to soften.

2. Warm mixture over low heat, stirring until gelatin dissolves.

3. In a large bowl, mix together pineapple, 1/4 cup pineapple juice, and apple concentrate. Thoroughly stir in gelatin mixture.

4. Chill until thickened but not set.

5. Fold in yogurt, and spoon pudding into dessert dishes. Chill until set. Serve within several hours after combining yogurt or it may separate.

Yield: 6 servings

	RCU	FU	Cal	%Fat	P	F	C	Na
Per Serving	0	0	111	2	5	T	23	49

1 Serving = 1 Fruit exchange; 1/2 Milk exchange

BANANA PUDDING

You'll love this great-tasting non-dairy pudding!

2¼	C	unsweetened pineapple juice
1	T	frozen unsweetened apple juice concentrate, thawed
5	T	cornstarch
2	lg	ripe bananas

1. Place all ingredients into a blender container; blend until smooth.

2. Pour mixture into a saucepan; cook over medium heat until thickened, stirring constantly.

3. Variation: slice 2 bananas into 5 dessert dishes and distribute pudding evenly over the top of the bananas.

Yield: 1 English trifle or 6 pudding servings

	RCU	FU	Cal	%Fat	P	F	C	Na
Per Serving	0	0	150	3	1	.5	37	2

1 Serving = 2 Fruit exchange

BREAD PUDDING

This is a very sweet version of everyone's favorite bread pudding. You will never know the sugar is missing.

2	lg	eggs
2	lg	egg whites
4	slices	whole-grain bread, crust removed
½	C	raisins
1	C	skim milk
1	C	frozen unsweetened apple juice concentrate, thawed
1	tsp	vanilla

1. Cut bread into sixteen squares per slice. Set aside.

2. Beat eggs and egg whites; add apple juice concentrate.

3. Scald milk in double boiler until a scum forms; add slowly to the egg mixture. Add vanilla.

4. Pour egg mixture into a 1 1/2-quart baking dish that has been sprayed with nonstick vegetable coating. Press bread into the egg mixture; add raisins.

5. Bake at 350° until custard is thick and bread is browned (about 45 minutes).

Yield: 8 servings

	RCU	FU	Cal	%Fat	P	F	C	Na
Per Serving	0	0	142	12	5	2	29	116

1 Serving = 1 1/2 Fruit exchange; 1/2 Bread exchange

APPLE BREAD PUDDING

A very good version of the traditional bread pudding. This is a very moist custard dessert.

2	lg	eggs
2	lg	egg whites
1	12-oz can	evaporated skim milk
¾	C	frozen unsweetened apple juice concentrate, thawed
1	tsp	vanilla
1	lg	Red Delicious apple, peeled, cored, and grated
4	slices	whole-wheat bread, crust removed
½	C	raisins
		cinnamon

1. Remove bread crusts and cut bread into sixteen squares per slice. Set aside.

2. Beat eggs and egg whites; add apple juice concentrate.

3. Scald milk in double boiler until a scum forms; add slowly to the egg mixture. Add vanilla and grated apple.

4. Pour egg mixture into a 1 1/2-quart baking dish that has been sprayed with nonstick vegetable coating. Press bread into egg mixture; add raisins. Sprinkle top lightly with cinnamon.

5. Bake at 350° until custard is thick and bread is browned lightly (about 45 minutes).

Yield: 8 servings

	RCU	FU	Cal	%Fat	P	F	C	Na
Per Serving	0	0	171	11	7	2	32	146

1 Serving = 1 1/2 Fruit exchange; 1/2 Bread exchange; 1/2 Milk exchange

PUMPKIN BREAD PUDDING

You'll love this deliciously different version of bread pudding!

2	lg	egg whites
2	lg	eggs
1	C	pumpkin
½	tsp	cinnamon
¼	tsp	ground ginger
⅛	tsp	ground cloves
1	12-oz can	evaporated skim milk
¾	C	frozen unsweetened apple juice concentrate, thawed
4	slices	whole-wheat bread, crusts removed
½	C	raisins

1. Remove bread crusts and cut bread into sixteen squares per slice. Set aside.

2. Beat eggs and egg whites; add pumpkin and spices. Beat well.

3. Add apple juice concentrate and blend well.

4. Scald milk in double boiler until a scum forms; add slowly to egg mixture.

5. Pour egg mixture into a 1 1/2-quart baking dish that has been sprayed with nonstick vegetable coating. Press bread into egg mixture; add raisins.

6. Bake at 350° until custard is thick and bread is browned lightly (about 40 to 45 minutes).

Yield: 8 servings

	RCU	FU	Cal	%Fat	P	F	C	Na
Per Serving	0	0	166	11	7	2	31	148

1 Serving = 1 Fruit exchange; 1/2 Bread exchange; 1/2 Milk exchange

FRUITED BREAD PUDDING

A different twist to the traditional bread pudding.

2	lg	eggs
2	lg	egg whites
4	slices	whole-wheat bread, crust removed
¼	C	chopped dates
1	8-oz can	crushed pineapple, drained
1¼	C	evaporated skim milk
¾	C	frozen unsweetened apple juice concentrate, thawed
½	tsp	vanilla
		cinnamon

1. Remove bread crusts and cut bread into sixteen squares per slice. Set aside.

2. Beat eggs and egg whites; add apple concentrate and mix well.

3. Scald milk until a scum forms; add to egg mixture.

4. Stir in vanilla, dates, and drained pineapple.

5. Pour mixture into a 1 1/2-quart baking dish; press bread cubes into liquid until covered.

6. Sprinkle lightly with ground cinnamon. Bake at 350° for 45 minutes.

Yield: 8 servings

	RCU	FU	Cal	%Fat	P	F	C	Na
Per Serving	0	0	146	12	5.3	2	28	115

1 Serving = 1 Fruit exchange; 1/2 Bread exchange

BROWN RICE PUDDING

A delicious way to use leftover rice.

2	lg	eggs
2	lg	egg whites
¾	C	frozen unsweetened apple juice concentrate, thawed
½	tsp	vanilla
1	12-oz can	evaporated skim milk
1½	C	cooked brown rice
¼	C	raisins

1. Beat eggs and egg whites. Add apple juice concentrate and vanilla. Mix well.

2. Stir in evaporated milk until well blended. Add rice and raisins.

3. Pour into a 1 1/2-quart baking dish that has been sprayed with nonstick vegetable coating. Bake at 350° for 40 minutes.

Yield: 6 Servings

	RCU	FU	Cal	%Fat	P	F	C	Na
Per Serving	0	0	205	10	9	2	37	237

1 Serving = 1 Fruit exchange; 1/2 Bread exchange; 1/2 Milk exchange

QUICK TAPIOCA PUDDING

This will be a favorite of tapioca lovers.

3	T	quick-cooking tapioca
1	lg	beaten egg
2¼	C	skim milk
¾	C	frozen unsweetened apple juice concentrate, thawed
½	tsp	vanilla

1. Combine tapioca, egg, and apple concentrate in a saucepan. Slowly pour in milk and blend well.

2. Let stand for 5 minutes.

3. Bring to a full boil, stirring constantly. Remove from heat.

4. Stir in vanilla extract. Stir once after 20 minutes. Refrigerate until firm.

Yield: 6 (1/2-cup) servings

	RCU	FU	Cal	%Fat	P	F	C	Na
Per Serving	0	0	120	9	4	1	23	68

1 Serving = 1 Fruit exchange; 1/2 Milk exchange

PINEAPPLE-BANANA PUDDING

Easy, fast, and delicious!

1	8-oz can	unsweetened crushed pineapple
2	lg	ripe bananas
1	C	evaporated skim milk
⅓	C	frozen unsweetened pineapple-orange-banana concentrate
½	tsp	vanilla
¼	tsp	banana extract
2	T	cornstarch

1. Combine all ingredients in blender container; process until smooth.

2. Pour into saucepan and cook over medium heat stirring constantly until mixture comes to a boil.

3. Remove from heat; pour into 6 dessert dishes. Refrigerate and serve when cool.

Yield: 6 servings

	RCU	FU	Cal	%Fat	P	F	C	Na
Per Serving	0	0	164	3	4	T	38	51

1 Serving = 2 Fruit exchange; 1/2 Milk exchange

Chapter Six

Frozen Desserts

Frozen Desserts

Ice cream is notoriously high in fat. The smooth, creamy richness of gourmet ice cream, in fact, is primarily due to the cream and eggs it's made of. We might enjoy it, but commercially manufactured ice cream isn't a very good option if you're watching the fats and cholesterol in your diet in an attempt to achieve better health or weight control.

If you especially look forward to frozen treats on the hot days of summer, these recipes are what you've been looking for! Although there is no substitution for ice cream, there are plenty of other healthful frozen treats. Sorbet is a smooth and refreshing fruit ice. Frozen yogurts are becoming increasingly popular, and some homemade versions are included here. The Frozen Blueberry Yogurt is a recipe that the teenagers in my home love to make-- it's fast and easy with a minimum of cleanup.

The Pineapple "Sherbet" is one you will want to try--even those who were sure they wouldn't like it ended up eating the whole batch. Best of all, it doesn't get much easier than in this recipe.

There are a variety of ice cream freezers available on the market, and they're a big switch from the cumbersome old-timers that required pounds of ice and salt. Try one of the newer models: some, either electric or hand-turned, have cores that you freeze and that require no ice at all (they're great for taking on a picnic!). Others, either electric or hand-turned, are small enough to sit on your kitchen counter and require a minimum of ice and salt. Check into all the options available, and you can greatly expand your dessert-making options.

FROZEN BLUEBERRY YOGURT

This is a sweet spectacular ending for any meal, or a perfect refresher for a warm summer afternoon. Even your devoted sugar fans will like this one.

2	C	plain nonfat yogurt
1	C	frozen unsweetened blueberries
¾	C	frozen unsweetened apple juice concentrate, thawed
1	T	frozen unsweetened orange juice concentrate, thawed
1	tsp	vanilla

1. Place all ingredients in blender container; puree until smooth.

2. Pour into ice cream freezer container; freeze according to manufacturer's instructions.

Yield: 6 (1/2-cup) servings

	RCU	FU	Cal	%Fat	P	F	C	Na
Per Serving	0	0	121	3	5	T	25	59

1 Serving = 1 Fruit exchange; 1/2 Milk exchange

FROZEN YOGURT

A smooth, tangy "sherbet-like" dessert.

2	med	ripe bananas
2	C	plain nonfat yogurt
1½	C	frozen unsweetened pineapple-orange-banana concentrate, thawed
1	tsp	vanilla

1. Puree the bananas, yogurt, juice concentrate, and vanilla in a blender.

2. Pour into the container of an ice cream freezer and freeze, following manufacturer's directions.

Yield: 8 (1/2-cup) servings

	RCU	FU	Cal	%Fat	P	F	C	Na
Per Serving	0	0	145	2	4	T	32	46

1 Serving = 2 Fruit exchange; 1/2 Milk exchange

FROZEN ORANGE YOGURT

A tangy orange-flavored frozen yogurt.

2	C	plain nonfat yogurt
¾	C	frozen unsweetened orange juice concentrate, thawed
1	tsp	vanilla

1. Combine all ingredients until smooth.

2. Pour into ice cream freezer can. Freeze according to manufacturer's instructions.

Yield: 5 (1/2-cup) servings

	RCU	FU	Cal	%Fat	P	F	C	Na
Per Serving	0	0	108	2	6	T	20	71

1 Serving = 1 Fruit exchange; 1/2 Milk exchange

PINEAPPLE "SHERBET"

This sherbet-like dessert is sure to please everyone in your family. Very easy to prepare and very delicious.

1	20-oz can	unsweetened pineapple chunks, drained, juice reserved
⅓	C	skim milk
½	tsp	vanilla

1. Spread out pineapple chunks on a cookie sheet so none touch each other. Freeze until chunks are hard.

2. When ready to serve, drop chunks into a blender container; add milk and reserved 3/4 cup pineapple juice.

3. Process about 30 seconds or until mixture is smooth.

4. Serve immediately.

Yield: 6 (1/2-cup) servings

	RCU	FU	Cal	%Fat	P	F	C	Na
Per Serving	0	0	63	2	1	T	16	9

1 Serving = 1 Fruit exchange

PEAR SHERBET AND BERRIES

Very refreshing light summer dessert.

2	16-oz cans	pear halves in fruit concentrate, undrained
¼	C	evaporated skim milk
¼	C	frozen unsweetened apple juice concentrate
1	C	fresh sliced strawberries
1	C	fresh blueberries

1. Drain pears, reserving 3/4 cup liquid.

2. Cut pears into 1-inch cubes; place on a baking sheet and freeze until firm (about 2 hours).

3. Place pears in blender container; cover and process about 2 minutes. Add reserved pear liquid, evaporated milk, and apple juice concentrate; process until smooth.

4. Pour mixture into a 9" x 9" pan. Freeze until firm, stirring every 30 minutes.

5. To serve, spoon pear mixture into 8 individual dessert dishes. Combine berries and spoon over pear sherbet.

Yield: 8 (1/2-cup) servings

	RCU	FU	Cal	%Fat	P	F	C	Na
Per Serving	0	0	92	3	1	T	23	17

1 Serving = 1 1/2 Fruit exchange

PINEAPPLE FREEZE

This is a very tasty sherbet-like dessert. If it gets frozen, simply remove it from the freezer for a few hours before serving; serve it when it's soft and icy.

1½	C	plain nonfat yogurt
1¼	C	unsweetened crushed pineapple, drained
1	T	lemon juice
¼	tsp	coconut extract
2	T	frozen unsweetened pineapple juice concentrate

1. Place all ingredients in a blender; blend until smooth.

2. Place the mixture in a bowl and put it in the freezer. Stir occasionally so that no ice crystals form.

Yield: 6 (1/2-cup) servings

	RCU	FU	Cal	%Fat	P	F	C	Na
Per Serving	0	0	75	2	4	T	16	45

1 Serving = 1/2 Fruit exchange; 1/2 Milk exchange

BLUEBERRY "ICE CREAM"

A creamy smooth, easy frozen dessert that will be a great ending to any meal.

3	C	frozen blueberries (approximately 3/4 package)
1¼	C	evaporated skim milk
½	C	frozen raspberries
3	T	frozen unsweetened pineapple juice concentrate,
3	T	frozen unsweetened apple juice concentrate,

1. Combine all ingredients in a blender container; blend until smooth and creamy. Serve immediately.

Yield: 8 (1/2-cup) servings

	RCU	FU	Cal	%Fat	P	F	C	Na
Per Serving	0	0	88	5	3	.5	18	48

1 Serving = 1 Fruit exchange; 1/3 Milk exchange

STRAWBERRY SORBET

This is a delicious refreshing sherbet-like dessert that's a particular favorite with children!

3	C	sliced fresh strawberries
1½	C	unsweetened pineapple juice
½	C	frozen unsweetened apple juice concentrate
1	lg	egg white (room temperature)

1. Combine strawberries, pineapple juice, and apple juice concentrate in a blender container; process until smooth.

2. Pour pureed mixture into a large bowl; set aside.

3. Beat egg white until stiff peaks form. Stir one-fourth of beaten egg white into reserved strawberry mixture, then fold in the remaining egg white gently but thoroughly.

4. Pour strawberry mixture into freezer can of a 1-gallon ice cream freezer. Freeze according to manufacturer's instructions.

Yield: 2 quarts or 12 (3/4-cup) servings

	RCU	FU	Cal	%Fat	P	F	C	Na
Per Serving	0	0	49	4	1	T	18	8

1 Serving = 1 Fruit exchange

WATERMELON SORBET

This is a fun--and refreshing--way to use watermelon!

4	C	watermelon, peeled, seeded, and cubed
4	lg	ice cubes
¼	C	frozen unsweetened apple juice concentrate

1. Place all ingredients in blender container; blend until smooth.

2. Pour into container of electric ice cream freezer and freeze until firm, following manufacturer's directions.

Yield: 4 servings

	RCU	FU	Cal	%Fat	P	F	C	Na
Per Serving	0	0	80	8	1	1	19	8

1 Serving = 1 Fruit exchange

PEACH SORBET

Another delicious treat for fresh peach season!

7	med	fresh peaches, peeled, pitted, and sliced
2	T	frozen unsweetened orange juice concentrate
¾	C	frozen unsweetened apple juice concentrate
2	lg	egg whites (room temperature)

1. Combine peach slices, orange juice, and apple juice concentrate in blender container; cover and process until smooth.

2. Beat egg whites until stiff peaks form. Stir one-fourth of egg whites into peach mixture; fold in remaining whites gently but thoroughly.

3. Pour mixture into can of a 1-gallon ice cream freezer. Freeze according to manufacturer's instructions.

Yield: 1 quart or 8 (1/2-cup) servings

	RCU	FU	Cal	%Fat	P	F	C	Na
Per Serving	0	0	82	2	2	T	20	19

1 Serving = 1 Fruit exchange

FRESH PEACH ICE

Great way to use fresh peaches--smooth and cool.

5	C	peeled and sliced peaches (about 3 pounds)
⅔	C	ripe banana, mashed
½	C	frozen unsweetened apple juice concentrate
2	T	lemon juice
1	lg	unpeeled fresh peach, thinly sliced

1. Combine first four ingredients in blender container. Cover and process until smooth.

2. Pour mixture into ice cream freezer container; freeze according to manufacturer's instructions.

3. To serve: Place three peach slices in dessert bowl and top with a scoop of peach ice.

Yield: 8 (1/2-cup) servings

	RCU	FU	Cal	%Fat	P	F	C	Na
Per Serving	0	0	107	3	1	T	27	5

1 Serving = 1 1/2 Fruit exchange

KIWI ICE

This cool and refreshing dessert is a fun way to use the kiwifruit.

4		kiwifruit, peeled and cubed
½	C	frozen unsweetened pineapple juice concentrate
½	C	frozen unsweetened apple juice concentrate
1	C	water
1	T	lemon juice

1. Combine ingredients in a blender; blend until smooth.

2. Pour mixture into an 8" x 8" baking pan; freeze until almost firm (about 1 hour).

3. Beat frozen mixture until fluffy. Return to pan and freeze until firm.

Yield: 4 cups or 4 (1-cup) servings

	RCU	FU	Cal	%Fat	P	F	C	Na
Per Serving	0	0	171	3	1	T	42	14

1 Serving = 2 1/2 Fruit exchange

Chapter Seven

Fruit Desserts

Fruit Desserts

If you savor the sweet aroma of ripened fruit, you'll love these recipes for cooked fruit as well as fresh fruit desserts. Warm fruit desserts are a real treat on a cool autumn or winter day, and can be a simple part of meal preparation. When you oven-bake your dinner, simply throw in a recipe or two of baked apples at the same time--your house will smell deliriously wonderful.

Many people think that fresh fruit for dessert just isn't dessert. These recipes prove otherwise! The recipes provided take fruit beyond just eating an apple or orange at the end of a meal. The combinations are delicious--and during fresh fruit season, they are economical besides!

BAKED APPLES

Great tasting baked apples. When you prepare an oven-baked meal, throw in a recipe--saves on preparation time .

4	sm	baking apples
2	T	wheat germ
2	T	raisins
¼	tsp	cinnamon
¼	C	chopped walnuts, optional
1	C	frozen unsweetened apple juice concentrate, thawed

1. Preheat oven to 350°.

2. Core apples; peel about 1/4 of the way down.

3. Arrange apples in a baking dish that has been sprayed with nonstick vegetable coating.

4. Combine wheat germ, raisins, cinnamon, and walnuts. Fill centers of apples with mixture.

5. Drizzle apple juice over apples.

6. Bake about 45 minutes or until tender.

Yield: 4 servings

	RCU	FU	Cal	%Fat	P	F	C	Na
Per Serving	0	0	107	5	T	T	28	6

1 Serving = 1 1/2 Fruit exchange

CRUNCHY BAKED APPLES

These will make a great ending to any meal--especially in the fall and winter.

4	med	cooking apples
¼	C	frozen unsweetened apple juice concentrate, thawed
1	tsp	ground cinnamon
3	T	Grape Nuts
¼	C	plain nonfat yogurt

1. Core apples 3/4 through; peel top 1/3 of each apple. Place apples in an 8" x 8" baking dish that has been sprayed with nonstick vegetable coating.

2. Place 1 tablespoon apple juice concentrate in each apple cavity. Add 1/4 teaspoon cinnamon on top of juice.

3. Add 1/2 cup water to baking dish. Cover and bake at 350° for 45 minutes.

4. Remove from oven; spoon 2 teaspoons cereal in each apple.

Yield: 4 servings

	RCU	FU	Cal	%Fat	P	F	C	Na
Per Serving	0	0	139	4	2	T	34	53

1 Serving = 2 Fruit exchange

BAKED PEARS AND APPLES

A very easy and tasty dessert. Great to make if you are using your oven for dinner.

⅓	C	water
⅓	C	frozen unsweetened apple juice concentrate, thawed
2	T	lemon juice
¾	tsp	cinnamon
3	med	apples, peeled, cored, and cut in half
3	med	pears, peeled, cored, and cut in half

1. Mix water, apple juice, lemon juice, and cinnamon.

2. Placed halved apples and pears in a single layer in a baking dish that has been sprayed with nonstick vegetable coating. Pour the juice mixture over the fruit.

3. Cover the baking dish; bake until the fruit is tender, about 30 to 35 minutes at 350°.

4. Place an apple half and a pear half in a dessert dish for each serving. Pour some of the liquid on top of each serving.

Yield: 6 servings

	RCU	FU	Cal	%Fat	P	F	C	Na
Per Serving	0	0	113	5	.5	.6	29	5

1 Serving = 2 Fruit exchange

POACHED APPLES

This great-tasting, easy dessert can be served with Banana Cream.

4	lg	red cooking apples
½	C	Smucker's Cranberry Fruit Blend juice (no sugar added)
¼	C	frozen unsweetened apple juice concentrate, thawed

1. Core apples. Slice each apple crosswise into thirds (fourths if a large apple). Arrange apples in a microwave-safe dish that has been sprayed with nonstick vegetable coating.

2. Combine juice and apple concentrate; pour over apples.

3. Microwave, covered, on high for 5 to 7 minutes or until tender. Spoon liquid over apples once during cooking.

4. Serve immediately with Banana Cream (see recipe Chapter 11).

Yield: 4 servings

	RCU	FU	Cal	%Fat	P	F	C	Na
Per Serving	0	0	165	4.5	.5	.8	42	8

1 Serving = 2 1/2 Fruit exchange

BAR-B-QUED BAKED APPLES

An easy and tasty accompaniment to your favorite outdoor meal.

¼	C	raisins
¼	C	chopped walnuts, optional
4	lg	apples, cored
¾	C	frozen unsweetened apple juice concentrate, thawed

1. Combine raisins and walnuts. Fill each apple with 2 tablespoons of the mixture.

2. Place each apple on aluminum foil. Bring the corners to the center. Place 3 tablespoons of apple juice concentrate into each foil packet; twist center corners to seal.

3. Grill about 6 inches from the coals for 20 minutes. Turn once during cooking.

Yield: 4 servings

	RCU	FU	Cal	%Fat	P	F	C	Na
Per Serving	0	0	196	3.3	.8	.7	50	15

1 Serving = 3 Fruit exchange

FRUIT CRISP

A very easy dessert that can be made ahead of time. The combination of fruit and carob chips makes for an interesting flavor. Serve in small dessert bowls.

1	med	pear
1	med	banana
1	lg	apple, peeled and cored
¼	C	chopped dates
⅛	C	unsweetened carob chips, optional
¼	C	frozen unsweetened apple juice concentrate, thawed
1	C	granola (see recipe chapter 9)
½	tsp	cinnamon

1. Cut fruit into bite-sized pieces; arrange in an 8" x 8" baking dish that has been sprayed with nonstick vegetable coating.

2. Sprinkle carob chips over the fruit.

3. Drizzle apple juice concentrate over the fruit mixture.

4. Mix cinnamon into the granola; sprinkle the granola mixture over the fruit mixture.

5. Bake at 350° for 25 minutes.

Yield: 6 servings

	RCU	FU	Cal	%Fat	P	F	C	Na
Per Serving	0	0	157	6	3	1	37	6

1 Serving = 2 Fruit exchange; 1/2 Bread exchange

JEWELED CRISP

A quick and easy dessert your entire family will enjoy.

2	16-oz can	no-sugar-added fruit cocktail, drained (save juice)
½	C	frozen unsweetened apple juice concentrate, thawed
2	T	cornstarch
1	tsp	finely grated orange peel
1	tsp	vanilla
¼	tsp	pumpkin pie spice
1	C	granola (see recipe chapter 9)

1. Drain fruit, reserving 1/2 cup liquid. Whisk together reserved liquid, 1/2 cup apple juice concentrate, cornstarch, orange peel, vanilla, and pumpkin pie spice.

2. Place in 9" x 9" glass baking dish that has been sprayed with nonstick vegetable coating. Microwave on high power for 4 minutes, stirring after 2 minutes. Remove dish from oven and stir in fruit.

3. Sprinkle granola over top of fruit mixture. Microwave on high power 6 minutes, rotating dish after 3 minutes. Remove from oven and cool.

Yield: 8 servings

	RCU	FU	Cal	%Fat	P	F	C	Na
Per Serving	0	0	145	12	2.6	2	31	10

1 Serving = 1 1/2 Fruit exchange; 1/2 Bread exchange

FRUIT COMPOTE

This is a great autumn or winter treat!

1	lb	pitted dried prunes
½	lb	dried apricots
1	16-oz can	unsweetened pineapple chunks, drained
1	16-oz can	sliced peaches in juice concentrate (no sugar), drained
8	oz	frozen unsweetened pitted sweet cherries
½	C	frozen unsweetened apple juice concentrate, thawed
¼	C	water

1. Soak prunes and apricots in enough water to cover them for 1 hour.

2. Drain the dried fruit and the canned fruit.

3. In a 9" x 13" baking dish that has been sprayed with nonstick vegetable coating, layer the fruit, ending with the cherries.

4. Combine apple juice concentrate and water; pour over fruit.

5. Cover and bake at 350° for 50 to 60 minutes.

Yield: 20 servings

	RCU	FU	Cal	%Fat	P	F	C	Na
Per Serving	0	0	124	2.4	1	T	32	5

1 Serving = 2 Fruit exchange

PEAR GOODIE

A soft bar-like dessert that you will want to eat with a fork. Delicious served warm or cold, it's a great way to take advantage of the fresh pear season. I usually use Bartlett pears for this recipe.

2	lg	egg whites
¼	C	frozen unsweetened apple juice concentrate, thawed
½	C	whole wheat flour
1	tsp	baking powder
2	lg	ripe pears, peeled and cut into 1/2" pieces
¼	C	chopped walnuts, optional
1	tsp	vanilla

1. Beat egg whites and apple juice concentrate until light.

2. Fold in flour and baking powder.

3. Fold in pears, walnuts, and vanilla.

4. Place in an 8" x 8" pan that has been sprayed with nonstick vegetable coating.

5. Bake at 350° for 30 minutes.

6. Serve hot or cold.

7. Grape Nuts cereal may be used in place of nuts.

Yield: 6 servings

	RCU	FU	Cal	%Fat	P	F	C	Na
Per Serving	0	0	110	5	3	T	25	72

1 Serving = 1 Fruit exchange; 1/2 Bread exchange

FRUIT DESSERT

A light delicious combination of fruit.

1½	C	sliced strawberries
1½	C	raspberries
2	med	pears, cored and diced
2	lg	oranges, sectioned and cut into bite-size pieces
1	C	frozen unsweetened orange juice concentrate, thawed
½	tsp	lemon juice
½	tsp	vanilla

1. Combine fruit. Combine juices and vanilla extract. Pour over the fruit; blend well. Chill and serve in individual bowls.

Yield: 6 (1-cup) servings

	RCU	FU	Cal	%Fat	P	F	C	Na
Per Serving	0	0	100	5	1	T	25	2

1 Serving = 1 1/2 Fruit exchange

SUMMERTIME FRUIT DESSERT

Great light combination of fruit with an easy sauce.

2	C	fresh blueberries
2	lg	bananas, sliced
2	C	sliced in half fresh strawberries
2	C	seedless green grapes
2		nectarines, unpeeled and sliced
2	lg	peaches, peeled and sliced
2		kiwi, peeled and sliced

1. Layer fruit in serving bowl. Just before serving, pour Orange Sauce over fruit.

Yield: 12 (1-cup) servings

Orange Sauce:

⅓	C	frozen unsweetened orange juice concentrate, thawed
2	T	lemon juice
2	T	frozen unsweetened pineapple juice concentrate, thawed
	dash	nutmeg

1. Combine all ingredients in a bowl and mix well. Chill.

	RCU	FU	Cal	%Fat	P	F	C	Na
Per Serving	0	0	86	5	1	T	21	3

1 Serving = 1 1/2 Fruit exchange

AMBROSIA

A tasty dessert or accompaniment to any meal.

2	med	oranges, peeled, with white removed
1	sm	banana, peeled, cut into small slices
20		seedless green or red grapes, cut in half
1		pink grapefruit, peeled, with white removed
1	C	strawberries, cut in half
⅓	C	frozen unsweetened orange juice concentrate, thawed
1	tsp	lemon juice
¼	C	unsweetened coconut, optional

1. Cut oranges and grapefruit into small pieces. In a large bowl, combine all ingredients and toss well.

Yield: 8 servings

	RCU	FU	Cal	%Fat	P	F	C	Na
Per Serving	0	0	56	4	1	.3	14	1

1 Serving = 1 Fruit exchange

AMBROSIA FRUIT CUP

The dates give this dessert ambrosia a delightfully different, sweet flavor.

1	lg	apple, red or green, not peeled
1	lg	banana
1	lg	orange, peeled and sectioned
6–10		dates, pitted and chopped
2	T	unsweetened coconut (optional)

1. Remove all white parts and membranes of each orange section over a bowl, reserving juice to pour over all the fruit.

2. Core and cube the apple. Cut the banana lengthwise and then cut into small pieces.

3. Mix all the fruit thoroughly with reserved orange juice. The orange juice keeps the bananas and apples from darkening. Chill.

4. Divide into four dessert bowls and sprinkle with coconut, if desired.

Yield: 4 servings

	RCU	FU	Cal	%Fat	P	F	C	Na
Per Serving	0	0	132	3	1.3	.4	34	2

1 Serving = 2 Fruit exchange

PINEAPPLE FRUIT DELIGHT

This recipe not only looks nice, but tastes great with the yogurt dressing.

1	lg	fresh pineapple
3	lg	oranges
2		pears, peeled, cored, and diced
1¼	C	seedless grapes, cut in half

Yogurt Dressing

1. Cut pineapple in half lengthwise. Leave the shell 1/2" thick. Remove the core and cut pineapple into small chunks.

2. Peel and section the oranges.

3. Combine fruits and spoon into pineapple shells. Top with Yogurt Dressing.

Yogurt Dressing:

1	C	nonfat plain yogurt
¼	C	frozen unsweetened pineapple-orange juice concentrate, thawed
¼	tsp	ground ginger (or to taste)

1. Mix and chill.

Yield: 6 servings

	RCU	FU	Cal	%Fat	P	F	C	Na
Per Serving	0	0	159	4	4	1	38	31

1 Serving = 2 Fruit exchange

SPARKLING FRUIT COMPOTE

This is a lovely and delicious light finish to any meal.

2	lg	Golden Delicious apples, unpeeled, chopped
1½	C	fresh or canned pineapple chunks
1	C	seedless red grapes, halved
3		kiwifruit, peeled and sliced
¾	C	sparkling apple cider, chilled
		fresh mint sprigs (optional)

1. Combine first three ingredients; toss gently. Cover with plastic wrap and chill.

2. Line 6 individual dessert dishes with kiwifruit. Divide apple mixture among the dessert dishes; drizzle 2 tablespoons of sparkling apple juice over each dish.

3. Garnish with mint sprigs, if desired. Serve immediately.

Yield: 6 servings

	RCU	FU	Cal	%Fat	P	F	C	Na
Per Serving	0	0	130	4	1	.6	33	6

1 Serving = 2 Fruit exchange

FRESH FRUIT KEBOBS

Serve these as either an attractive appetizer or a delicious dessert!

Bananas, sliced into bite-size pieces
Strawberries, washed and hulled
Kiwis, peeled and cut into 1/4-inch slices
Fresh pineapple, cut into chunks, or unsweetened pineapple chunks, drained (save juice)

Cantaloupe, cut into squares
Honeydew melon, cut into squares
Grapes

1. Dip banana pieces into pineapple juice.

2. Thread fruit alternately onto wooden skewers in any combination desired. Cover and chill.

BLUEBERRY FRUIT DIP

Cut a variety of fruits (such as canned pineapple chunks, bananas, grapes, cantaloupe, honeydew melon, watermelon, or strawberries) into bite-sized portions and arrange attractively on a tray. Place some of this dip on top of the fruit, or let your guests dip the fruit. This dip is sure to be a favorite with your family and guests.

¾	C	frozen blueberries
1	C	low-fat cottage cheese
2	sm	ripe bananas, peeled, sliced, and frozen
2	T	frozen unsweetened apple juice concentrate, thawed

1. Place cottage cheese in a blender and blend until smooth.

2. Add blueberries, bananas, and apple juice concentrate.

3. Cover and blend until smooth.

4. Cover and chill until serving time.

5. Serve with a variety of bite-sized fruit chunks as a dip or topping.

Yield: 8 (1/4-cup) servings

	RCU	FU	Cal	%Fat	P	F	C	Na
Per Serving	0	0	61	8	4	T	11	116

1 Serving = 1/2 Fruit exchange

GINGER FRUIT DIP

This is a tasty low-fat fruit dip.

1	C	low-fat cottage cheese
1	med	banana, cut into chunks
⅛	tsp	ground ginger
		frozen unsweetened apple juice concentrate, thawed

1. In a blender, combine the cottage cheese, banana, and ginger. Cover and blend until the mixture is smooth.

2. Blend in enough apple juice concentrate (about 1 tablespoon) to make the dip a desired consistency. Place dip in an airtight container; cover. Chill.

3. Serve with fruit slices (apple wedges, kiwi fruit slices, or no-sugar mandarin orange sections).

Yield: 1 1/4 cups or 5 (1/4-cup) servings

	RCU	FU	Cal	%Fat	P	F	C	Na
Per Serving	0	0	66	9	6	.6	10	185

1 Serving = 1/2 Fruit exchange

FRUIT MELBA

Sure to be enjoyed by raspberry lovers.

¼	C	frozen unsweetened apple-raspberry juice concentrate, thawed
¼	C	water
1	tsp	cornstarch
3	drops	almond extract
1	C	fresh or frozen unsweetened raspberries
3	C	cantaloupe balls

1. Combine juice concentrate and water in a saucepan. Add cornstarch and stir until combined.

2. Cook over medium heat, stirring constantly until mixture is thick and bubbly.

3. Remove sauce from heat and stir in almond extract. Cool.

4. Combine fruit and spoon into 6 dessert dishes.

5. Top with cooled sauce.

Yield: 6 servings

	RCU	FU	Cal	%Fat	P	F	C	Na
Per Serving	0	0	59	6	1	T	14	10

1 Serving = 1 Fruit exchange

STRAWBERRIES WITH RASPBERRY MELBA SAUCE

Light and attractive dessert.

2	C	fresh strawberries, stems removed
1½	C	fresh or thawed frozen raspberries
1	T	frozen unsweetened orange juice concentrate, thawed
2	T	frozen unsweetened apple juice concentrate, thawed

1. In a blender, combine raspberries, orange juice, and apple juice concentrate; cover and process until smooth.

2. Combine raspberry mixture and strawberries in a bowl; toss gently to coat. Cover and chill for 2 hours.

Yield: 4 (1/2-cup) servings

	RCU	FU	Cal	%Fat	P	F	C	Na
Per Serving	0	0	61	8	1	.6	15	3

1 Serving = 1 Fruit exchange

Chapter Eight

Shakes & Fruit Punch

Shakes & Fruit Punch

If you usually regard sweet-tasting drinks as drinks full of sugar, get ready for a pleasant surprise: this chapter provides you with healthy drinks that you can serve to a crowd as well as drinks you can make for a few on the spur of the moment. Instead of preparing a fruit-punch base that is almost totally sugar and food coloring, make some of the nutritious fruit juice punches in this chapter. You'll love the great taste!

Frozen fruit shakes are traditionally high in fat and high in sugar--mainly because they are usually made with ice cream. And you've probably seen recipes for shakes that are supposed to be "good for you"--they usually don't taste good, and are anything but sweet. The shakes in this chapter will be a pleasant surprise: not only are they sweet, but they taste good, too! Keep frozen fruit on hand so when the children come in hot and thirsty, you can prepare a real treat with a minimum of cleanup. There's a bonus, too: they are easy enough that your older children can prepare these themselves!

TRIPLE BERRY SHAKE

This shake delivers great taste and cool refreshment on a warm summer day. The children will never know it's good for them!

½	C	fresh or frozen* strawberries, sliced
½	C	fresh or frozen* blueberries
½	C	fresh or frozen* raspberries
½	C	skim milk
⅔	C	frozen unsweetened apple juice concentrate

1. Place all ingredients in blender; blend until smooth.

Frozen fruit makes a thicker shake.

Yield: 4 servings

	RCU	FU	Cal	%Fat	P	F	C	Na
Per Serving	0	0	111	4	2	.5	26	29

1 Serving = 1 1/2 Fruit exchange

CRANBERRY BANANA FROST

This frost is deliciously refreshing.

1	lg	banana
3	T	frozen unsweetened apple-cranberry juice concentrate
1	T	frozen unsweetened orange juice concentrate
6		ice cubes

1. In electric blender container, combine banana, juice concentrates, and ice cubes; blend until slushy-smooth.

2. Garnish with orange slices, split once from edge to center and placed on edge of serving glass.

Yield: 2 (6-ounce) servings

	RCU	FU	Cal	%Fat	P	F	C	Na
Per Serving	0	0	163	4	2	1	41	8

1 Serving = 2 1/2 Fruit exchange

FRUIT ICE

This fruit slush is very refreshing on a warm summer day.

10		ice cubes
½	C	skim milk
¼	C	frozen unsweetened apple juice concentrate
⅓	C	plain nonfat yogurt
½	C	fresh or frozen fruit (blueberries, strawberries, raspberries, boysenberries, or blackberries)
½	tsp	vanilla

1. Place all ingredients in blender. Blend until smooth.

2. Serve immediately.

Yield: 2 servings

	RCU	FU	Cal	%Fat	P	F	C	Na
Per Serving	0	0	120	4	5	T	24	69

1 Serving = 1 Fruit exchange; 1/2 Milk exchange

TROPICAL SLUSH

Slushes are the ultimate in warm-weather drinks. As a bonus, this one is good for you, too!

1	lg	banana
½	C	unsweetened crushed pineapple, undrained
3	T	frozen unsweetened pineapple-orange-banana concentrate
6		ice cubes

1. In electric blender container, combine banana, pineapple, juice concentrate, and ice cubes; blend until smooth.

2. Garnish with pineapple spear.

Yield: 2 (7-ounce) servings

	RCU	FU	Cal	%Fat	P	F	C	Na
Per Serving	0	0	192	3	2	.6	49	3

1 Serving = 3 Fruit exchange

FRUIT SLUSH

A cool, refreshing, good-for-you drink.

¾	C	frozen unsweetened Fruit-n-Berry or Apple-Raspberry juice concentrate
1	C	plain nonfat yogurt
1	lg	banana
3	C	ice cubes

1. Combine juice concentrate, yogurt, and banana in blender container; process until smooth.

2. Add ice cubes and process until thick and smooth.

Yield: 4 (1-cup) servings

	RCU	FU	Cal	%Fat	P	F	C	Na
Per Cup	0	0	172	3	4	.6	39	57

1 Cup = 3 Fruit exchange

ORANGE SLUSH

This frosty refresher is similar to the orange ice slush sold in major malls.

2	C	unsweetened orange juice
½	C	instant nonfat dry milk powder
½	tsp	vanilla extract
8–10		ice cubes

1. Combine all ingredients in blender; process until mixture is frothy. Serve immediately.

Yield: 4 (1-cup) servings

	RCU	FU	Cal	%Fat	P	F	C	Na
Per Cup	0	0	88	1	4	T	18	48

1 Cup = 1 Fruit exchange

SPARKLING PUNCH

This makes a delicious and attractive punch for any occasion. This was a favorite at many parties and family gatherings.

1	46-oz can	unsweetened pineapple juice, chilled
¾	C	unsweetened orange juice concentrate, thawed
1	28-oz bottle	club soda, chilled
1	sm	fresh lemon, thinly sliced
1	C	frozen raspberries

1. Immediately before serving, combine juice, orange juice concentrate, and club soda.

2. Garnish with lemon slices and frozen raspberries.

Yield: 3 quarts or 12 (1-cup) servings

	RCU	FU	Cal	%Fat	P	F	C	Na
Per Cup	0	0	88	2	1	T	21	16

1 Cup = 1 1/2 Fruit exchange

APPLE PUNCH

This delicious punch was the hit of our office Christmas party. Serve with the fruited ice ring for an elegant touch.

2	3-in.	cinnamon sticks
2	qts	unsweetened apple juice, chilled
2	C	unsweetened orange juice, chilled
2	25-oz bottles	sparkling apple cider, chilled

1. Combine cinnamon sticks and apple juice; chill 2 hours. Remove cinnamon sticks. Combine apple juice and remaining ingredients in large punch bowl.

Yield: 16 cups

	RCU	FU	Cal	%Fat	P	F	C	Na
Per Cup	0	0	111	2	T	T	27	15

1 Cup = 2 Fruit exchange

FRUIT ICE RING

This is a beautiful and festive addition to your punch bowl, especially during the Christmas holidays.

4	clusters red seedless grapes
4	fresh orange slices, sliced 1/4 inch thick
4	fresh lime slices, sliced 1/4 inch thick
1	green apple, cored and thinly sliced into wedges
1	red apple, cored and thinly sliced into wedges
	apple juice

1. Place crushed ice in the bottom of a ring mold that will fit in your punch bowl.

2. Arrange the fruit attractively over the crushed ice so that it sticks up above the ring of the ring mold and so that the colorful fruit skins face upward. (See color photo.)

3. Slowly and carefully pour unsweetened apple juice around the fruit almost to the top of the mold. If you pour too fast, your fruit may float.

4. Freeze overnight. To unmold, place mold in a large bowl of warm water for a few seconds. Right before serving, place ice ring, fruit side up, in a filled punch bowl.

CRIMSON PUNCH

Great-tasting bubbly drink.

1	12-oz frozen whole unsweetened strawberries bag
1	12-oz frozen unsweetened apple-cranberry juice concentrate, thawed can
1	33-oz club soda, chilled bottle

1. Combine strawberries and apple-cranberry concentrate in electric blender container. Cover and process until smooth.

2. Pour into a large pitcher; add club soda, stirring gently to blend.

3. Serve immediately.

Yield: 8 cups

	RCU	FU	Cal	%Fat	P	F	C	Na
Per Cup	0	0	102	2	T	T	25	39

1 Cup = 1 1/2 Fruit exchange

PINEAPPLE ICE PUNCH

Use this recipe to delight the guests at your next party.

1	20-oz can	unsweetened pineapple chunks, undrained
2	T	frozen unsweetened orange juice concentrate, thawed
2	32-oz cans	unsweetened pineapple juice, chilled
½	C	lemon juice
½	C	unsweetened orange juice
1	33-oz bottle	club soda or sparkling mineral water, chilled

1. Place pineapple chunks (including the liquid) and 2 T orange juice concentrate in a 9" x 13" pan; cover and freeze until firm.

2. Break up pineapple and place in blender container; cover and process until smooth. Place in freezer container; cover and freeze.

3. Combine 2 quarts pineapple juice, lemon juice, and 1/2 cup orange juice; stir well. Pour 3/4 cup mixture into 12 glasses.

4. To each glass, add 1/3 cup club soda or mineral water and 1 tablespoon frozen pineapple mixture. Serve immediately.

Yield: 12 (1-cup) servings

	RCU	FU	Cal	%Fat	P	F	C	Na
Per Cup	0	0	124	1	1	T	31	19

1 Cup = 2 Fruit exchange

Pictured: Fruit Kebobs, p. 114; Blueberry Dip, p. 115; Mixed Fruit Cookies, p. 4.

APPLE OR GRAPE "SODA"

The kids can safely have this type of "soda."

1	12-oz can	frozen unsweetened apple or grape concentrate
2	tsp	lemon or lime juice
36	oz	chilled club soda

1. Combine juices. Add club soda very slowly. Gently stir. Serve immediately over ice.

Yield: 6 (1-cup) servings

	RCU	FU	Cal	%Fat	P	F	C	Na
Per Serving	0	0	117	2	T	T	29	57

1 Cup = 2 Fruit exchange

JUICE REFRESHER

Very refreshing.

4	C	unsweetened apple juice
2	C	unsweetened pineapple juice
1	C	unsweetened orange juice
¼	C	lemon juice

1. Combine juices, stirring well. Chill. Before serving, garnish with mint sprigs, if desired.

Yield: 7 (1-cup) servings

	RCU	FU	Cal	%Fat	P	F	C	Na
Per Serving	0	0	119	1	1	0	29	11

1 Serving = 2 Fruit exchange

Pictured: Triple Berry Shake, p. 121; Tropical Slush, p. 123; Cranberry Banana Frost, p. 122; Apple Punch with Fruit Ring, p. 126.

CRANBERRY COCKTAIL

Serve this mildly spicy drink warm--it's especially great during the winter.

1		32-oz Smucker's unsweetened cranberry-flavored juice bottle
4		dried apricot halves, cut in fourths
3	T	cranberries, cut in half
4		whole cloves
1		stick cinnamon

1. Combine ingredients in saucepan; bring to a boil.

2. Cover, reduce heat, and simmer 10 minutes. Discard cloves and cinnamon.

3. Serve warm.

Yield: 6 (3/4-cup) servings

	RCU	FU	Cal	%Fat	P	F	C	Na
Per Serving	0	0	105	1	T	T	27	7

1 Serving = 2 Fruit exchange

Chapter Nine

Breakfast

Breakfast

Breakfast is a real dilemma for dieters--and for those who are changing to healthy eating habits. Traditional "breakfast" fare--such as bacon, sausage, ham, fried potatoes, eggs, donuts, sweet rolls, jam, maple syrup, and sugar-coated cereals--is high in both fat and sugar. Yet studies have shown that breakfast is a crucial meal. How can you strike a balance?

Easy!

This chapter provides plenty of ideas to get your day off to a healthy start. You'll find delicious jams and fruit syrups to pour over your pancakes, French toast, and waffles, as well as recipes for pancakes, French toast, and waffles that are delicious all by themselves.

You'll find some recipes for the out-of-the-ordinary, too. Give your children a breakfast fruit shake to accompany their cereal--or give them their juice in the form of a frozen popsicle on a hot summer day. They will be delighted!

So get on the breakfast crusade, and start with some new ideas. Don't make it difficult: prepare things in large batches and freeze them. Pancakes and waffles, as well as jams and fruit spreads, freeze beautifully!

BREAKFAST SHAKE

Great addition to any breakfast!

1	C	plain nonfat yogurt
1	lg	egg white
1	med	banana, sliced
¼	C	skim milk
½	C	unsweetened crushed pineapple, drained
¼	C	frozen unsweetened pineapple juice concentrate
1	tsp	vanilla

1. In blender, combine all ingredients. Blend at high speed for 30 seconds or until the mixture is smooth.

Yield: 4 (1/2-cup) servings

	RCU	FU	Cal	%Fat	P	F	C	Na
Per Serving	0	0	131	3	5	T	27	65

1 Serving = 1 Fruit exchange; 1/2 Milk exchange

GOOD MORNING DRINK

This delicious combination of fruit and nonfat dairy products makes a nutritious drink. This tastes too rich to be so low in calories!

1	C	fresh or frozen strawberries
1	sm	banana
¼	C	unsweetened crushed pineapple, slightly drained
1	C	skim milk
½	C	plain nonfat yogurt
¼	C	frozen unsweetened pineapple-orange juice concentrate, thawed
1	tsp	vanilla
¼	tsp	cinnamon

1. Combine all ingredients in a blender. Process until smooth.

Yield: 3 servings

	RCU	FU	Cal	%Fat	P	F	C	Na
Per Serving	0	0	161	4	6	T	34	73

1 Serving = 1 1/2 Fruit exchange; 1/2 Milk exchange

ORANGE SHAKE

This frosty way to serve orange juice will be a great addition to any breakfast!

1	C	skim milk
⅓	C	frozen unsweetened orange juice concentrate, thawed
1	tsp	vanilla
4		ice cubes

1. Combine all ingredients in blender container. Cover and process until smooth and frothy.

2. Serve immediately.

Yield: 2 servings

	RCU	FU	Cal	%Fat	P	F	C	Na
Per Serving	0	0	126	2	5	T	25	64

1 Serving = 1 Fruit exchange; 1/2 Milk exchange

BANANA BREAKFAST SMOOTHIE

A delicious and attractive breakfast drink--and a great way to include fruit in breakfast!

1	lg	ripe banana, peeled, cut into chunks, and frozen
1	C	fresh or unsweetened pineapple chunks, frozen individually
1	C	strawberries, mashed
½	C	plain nonfat yogurt
½	C	skim milk

1. Place all ingredients in a blender container; blend until smooth. Serve immediately.

Yield: 2 servings

	RCU	FU	Cal	%Fat	P	F	C	Na
Per Serving	0	0	256	4	8	1	59	79

1 Serving = 3 Fruit exchange; 1/2 Milk exchange

FRUIT YOGURT

You'll want to serve this often--it not only tastes great, but it's good for you!

1	C	sliced banana
¼	C	crushed unsweetened pineapple, drained
1	tsp	vanilla
½	tsp	lemon juice
1	C	plain nonfat yogurt
1	C	sliced strawberries

1. Combine banana, pineapple, vanilla, and lemon juice in a blender; process until smooth. Pour into a bowl.

2. Stir in yogurt and strawberries; blend well. Chill.

Yield: 4 servings

	RCU	FU	Cal	%Fat	P	F	C	Na
Per Serving	0	0	126	4	4	.6	28	45

1 Serving = 1 1/2 Fruit exchange; 1/2 Milk exchange

TROPICAL FRUIT SALAD

Here's a simple, yet elegant, addition to any summer breakfast. A winter version could be made by substituting apples and bananas for the cantaloupe and strawberries.

1	lg	fresh pineapple
1		orange, peeled, sliced
1	C	cubed cantaloupe
1½	C	fresh strawberries
1	C	seedless red or green grapes
1		lime

1. Cut pineapple in half lengthwise through crown. Remove fruit with a curved knife, leaving shells intact. Core and chunk the pineapple.

2. Measure 2 cups pineapple chunks for the salad; combine with the remaining fruit except for the lime.

3. Squeeze the lime juice; toss with the fruit.

4. Spoon into pineapple shells to serve.

Yield: 6 servings

	RCU	FU	Cal	%Fat	P	F	C	Na
Per Serving	0	0	89	7	1	T	22	5

1 Serving = 1 Fruit exchange

BANANA FLAPJACKS

Sure to become a favorite with every family member; delicious served with strawberry syrup.

2	tsp	baking soda
2¼	C	buttermilk
2	C	whole wheat flour
2	lg	egg whites
1	T	melted margarine or butter
2	C	sliced bananas (about 4 medium bananas)

1. In large bowl dissolve baking soda in buttermilk.

2. Add flour, egg whites, and butter; stir lightly.

3. Batter should be streaky and lumpy.

4. Gently fold in bananas.

5. Drop by spoonfuls onto hot griddle that has been sprayed with nonstick vegetable coating. Turn when bubbles begin to break. Cook until golden brown.

Note: Batter may thicken as it sits. Thin with buttermilk if necessary.

6. Serve with Strawberry Syrup.

Yield: 18 (4-inch) pancakes or 6 servings (3 pancakes per serving)

	RCU	FU	Cal	%Fat	P	F	C	Na
Per 3 Pancakes	0	0	286	13	11	4	57	408

3 Pancakes = 1 1/2 Fruit exchange; 1 1/2 Bread exchange; 1/2 Fat exchange

APPLE PANCAKES

A good-tasting pancake. Serve with any of the spreads or syrups listed in this chapter.

1½	C	whole wheat flour
1	tsp	baking soda
½	tsp	baking powder
¾	C	skim milk
¼	C	frozen unsweetened apple juice concentrate, thawed
½	C	finely chopped apple, peeled and cored
1	lg	egg white

1. Combine flour, baking soda, and baking powder in large bowl; mix well.

2. Combine milk, apple juice concentrate, apple, and egg white; add to flour mixture and stir until smooth.

3. Spray griddle or skillet with nonstick vegetable cooking spray; place over medium heat until hot.

4. Spoon batter, 2 tablespoons at a time, onto griddle. Cook until browned; turn and cook other side until golden brown.

5. Repeat with remaining batter.

Yield: 20 (3-inch) pancakes

	RCU	FU	Cal	%Fat	P	F	C	Na
Per Pancake	0	0	87	5	3	T	19	115

3 Pancakes = 1 Fruit exchange; 2 1/2 Bread exchange

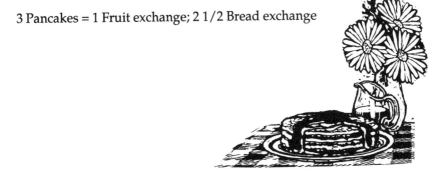

APPLE-FILLED PANCAKES

This will be a hit at your next brunch or family breakfast. The filling makes a great-tasting pancake. Make up extra filling and use as a topping for a cake.

Filling:

2	T	margarine or butter
6	C	apples, peeled, cored, and sliced 1/4-inch thick
1¼	tsp	cinnamon
1	C	frozen unsweetened apple juice concentrate, thawed

1. Melt butter in large skillet over moderate heat. Add apples and apple juice concentrate; sprinkle cinnamon over top of apples.

2. Cook until apples are tender and syrupy; set aside.

Pancake:

1½	C	whole wheat flour
2	tsp	baking powder
¼	C	frozen unsweetened apple juice concentrate, thawed
1	lg	egg white, beaten
1¼	C	skim milk
1	T	cold-pressed oil

1. Mix together flour and baking powder. Combine apple juice concentrate, egg white, milk, and oil; add to flour mixture all at once and stir just until blended.

2. Heat griddle over medium heat until a few drops of cold water will bounce in small beads before evaporating. Spray griddle with nonstick vegetable coating.

3. Pour a scant 1/4 cup batter onto griddle. Bake until center is full of unbroken bubbles. Turn and brown the other side.

4. To serve, place some of hot apple mixture in center of each pancake and roll up loosely. Place seam side down on heated plates.

Yield: 12 filled pancakes

	RCU	FU	Cal	%Fat	P	F	C	Na
Per pancake	0	0	81	17	3	2	14	71

3 Pancakes = 1/2 Fruit exchange; 2 Bread exchange; 1/2 Fat exchange

BANANA WAFFLES

What a great breakfast surprise! Serve with Strawberry Syrup, Banana Jam, or fresh sliced bananas with Strawberry Syrup.

3	C	whole wheat flour
4	tsp	baking powder
2	tsp	cinnamon
1	tsp	ground ginger
4	lg	egg whites
2	med	ripe bananas, pureed (1 cup)
1⅓	C	skim milk
¼	C	frozen unsweetened apple juice concentrate, thawed
¼	C	frozen unsweetened pineapple-orange-banana concentrate, thawed
2	T	cold-pressed oil

1. Preheat waffle iron. In a large bowl, combine flour, baking powder, cinnamon, and ginger.

2. In a mixing bowl, beat egg whites until light and fluffy. Beat in pureed banana, milk, juice concentrates, and oil; beat until light and fluffy.

3. Add egg mixture to dry ingredients; stir until just moistened. Bake in preheated waffle iron until golden brown.

Yield: 6 servings (1 waffle per serving)

	RCU	FU	Cal	%Fat	P	F	C	Na
Per Waffle	0	0	369	15	13	6	69	275

1 Waffle = 1 1/2 Fruit exchange; 2 1/2 Bread exchange; 1 Fat exchange

CINNAMON TOAST

A different breakfast idea.

4	slices	whole-grain bread
1	C	low-fat cottage cheese
4	T	unsweetened applesauce
		cinnamon

1. Toast bread. Spread 1 tablespoon applesauce on each slice.

2. Spread 1/4 cup cottage cheese on top of applesauce.

3. Sprinkle lightly with cinnamon.

4. Place cottage cheese toast under broiler until cheese is warm.

Yield: 2 servings (2 slices of toast per serving)

	RCU	FU	Cal	%Fat	P	F	C	Na
Per Serving	0	0	264	9	19	3	43	710

1 Serving = 1 Fruit exchange; 1 1/2 Bread exchange

FANCY FRENCH TOAST

A very hearty breakfast. Serve with fresh fruit or a fruit shake.

1	lg	egg
3	lg	egg whites
½	C	skim milk
½	tsp	vanilla
½	tsp	ground cinnamon
8	slices	whole-grain bread

1. Combine egg and egg whites; beat well. Add milk, vanilla, and cinnamon; stir until blended.

2. Dip bread slices, one at a time, into egg mixture, coating well; drain off the excess.

3. Coat a large skillet with nonstick cooking spray; place over low heat until hot. Arrange bread in a single layer in skillet and cook until browned on each side. Repeat with remaining bread slices.

4. Spoon 2 tablespoons of topping over each hot slice of bread. Garnish with fresh strawberries.

Topping:

1	C	low-fat cottage cheese
2	T	frozen unsweetened pineapple juice concentrate, thawed
2	T	frozen unsweetened apple juice concentrate, thawed
2	tsp	vanilla
1	tsp	lemon juice
½	tsp	cinnamon

1. Combine all ingredients in blender; process until smooth.

Yield: 4 servings (2 slices per serving)

	RCU	FU	Cal	%Fat	P	F	C	Na
Per Serving	0	0	236	13	17	4	35	545

1 Serving = 1/2 Fruit exchange; 1 1/2 Bread exchange

GRANOLA

A great-tasting no-fat, no-sugar granola. This recipe makes a great fruit cobbler topping--keep some on hand for a quick dessert.

4	C	rolled oats
4	C	rolled wheat
1	C	wheat germ
1	C	unroasted sunflower seeds, optional
¾	C	frozen unsweetened apple juice concentrate, thawed
2	tsp	vanilla
¾	C	chopped dates
¾	C	raisins
¾	C	dried apples, cut into bite-size pieces
1-2	C	slivered almonds, optional

1. Mix together oats, rolled wheat, and wheat germ. Add nuts if desired.

2. Combine apple juice concentrate and vanilla.

3. Blend all ingredients together; put into a 9" x 13" cake pan.

4. Bake at 275° for 1 hour.

5. After taking granola out of the oven, add the dried apples, dates, and raisins.

6. Use as a cold cereal or mix with nonfat plain yogurt and fruit for a delicious breakfast.

Yield: 12 cups or 16 (3/4-cup) servings

	RCU	FU	Cal	%Fat	P	F	C	Na
Per Serving	0	0	263	9	8	3	55	9

1 Serving = 1 1/2 Fruit; 2 Bread

CRUNCHY GRANOLA

This versatile recipe can be used in many ways. It may even be used in the Granola Muffin or Granola Cookie recipes as a substitute for regular granola.

1	C	rolled oats
¼	C	rolled wheat
½	C	coarsely chopped almonds
½	C	wheat germ
¼	C	chopped dates
¼	C	chopped dried apricots
¼	C	raisins
¾	tsp	cinnamon

1. Spread oats, almonds, and wheat germ in pan; bake at 350° for 8 minutes or until lightly toasted. Stir occasionally to keep from burning.

2. Cool completely. Combine oat mixture and remaining ingredients.

3. Store in an airtight container.

Yield: 3 cups or 6 (1/2-cup) servings

	RCU	FU	Cal	%Fat	P	F	C	Na
Per Serving	0	0	219	34	8	8	32	4

1 Serving = 1 Fruit exchange; 1 Bread exchange; 1 1/2 Fat exchange

CRUNCHY GRANOLA PARFAIT

This is a wonderful breakfast or brunch item.

½	C	sliced strawberries
½	C	plain nonfat yogurt
4	T	Crunchy Granola
1		kiwifruit, peeled and thinly sliced

1. In a tall parfait glass, place 1/4 cup strawberries; top with 2 tablespoons yogurt.

2. Sprinkle with 1 tablespoon Crunchy Granola. Top with half of kiwifruit; spoon 2 T yogurt over kiwifruit, and sprinkle with 1 T Crunchy Granola.

3. Repeat layers.

Yield: 1 serving

	RCU	FU	Cal	%Fat	P	F	C	Na
Per Serving	0	0	242	18	12	5	41	95

1 Serving = 1 1/2 Fruit exchange; 1/2 Bread exchange; 1 Milk exchange; 1 Fat exchange

CRUNCHY GRANOLA CEREAL

A slightly different easy version of a delicious hot cereal.

⅔	C	unsweetened apple juice or apricot nectar
⅔	C	water
⅔	C	Crunchy Granola
2	T	instant nonfat dry milk powder

1. Combine juice and water in saucepan; bring to a boil.

2. Add Crunchy Granola and dry milk; stir well. Cook 1 minute, stirring occasionally.

3. Remove from heat; cover and let stand 5 minutes. Serve immediately.

Yield: 2 (2/3-cup) servings

	RCU	FU	Cal	%Fat	P	F	C	Na
Per Serving	0	0	199	25	7	5	33	31

1 Serving = 1 Fruit exchange; 1 Bread exchange; 1 Fat exchange

APRICOT OATMEAL

You'll never go wrong with this cereal with its great taste!

1½	C	water
¼	C	frozen unsweetened apple juice concentrate, thawed
¾	C	quick-cooking rolled oats
¼	C	finely chopped dried apricots

1. Bring water and apple juice concentrate to a boil. Add oats and apricots; return to a boil.

2. Simmer until most of the liquid is absorbed. Remove from heat and cover; let sit for 5 minutes.

Yield: 2 servings

	RCU	FU	Cal	%Fat	P	F	C	Na
Per Serving	0	0	215	9	6	2	45	12

1 Serving = 1 1/2 Fruit exchange; 1 1/2 Bread exchange

FRUITED OATMEAL

A very delicious and unusual way to serve oatmeal. This doesn't need any added sugar or fruit.

2	C	unsweetened apple-cranberry juice
2	C	water
1¾	C	regular rolled oats
¼	C	instant nonfat dry milk powder
1	tsp	cinnamon
1	lg	Red Delicious apple, peeled, cored, and chopped

1. Combine juice and water in a medium pan; bring to a boil. Add the oats, dry milk, and cinnamon; cook about 8 minutes, stirring occasionally.

2. Remove from the heat and add the chopped apple. Cover and let stand for 6 minutes.

Yield: 5 (1-cup) servings

	RCU	FU	Cal	%Fat	P	F	C	Na
Per Serving	0	0	190	10	6	2	38	27

1 Serving = 1 Fruit exchange; 1 1/2 Bread exchange

BANANA JAM

A delicious jam to use on toast, pancakes, waffles, or as a topping for a cake.

¼	C	frozen unsweetened pineapple juice concentrate, thawed
½	C	frozen unsweetened apple juice concentrate, thawed
2	T	cornstarch
3	C	sliced ripe bananas
3	T	lemon juice

1. Combine thawed juice concentrates and cornstarch in saucepan; stir until smooth. Mash bananas.

2. Add remaining ingredients, stirring well. Cook over medium heat, stirring constantly, until thickened. Cool. Store in refrigerator.

Yield: 2 cups or 32 (1-tablespoon) servings

	RCU	FU	Cal	%Fat	P	F	C	Na
Per Tablespoon	0	0	40	4	T	T	10	1

2 Tablespoons = 1 Fruit exchange

STRAWBERRY SPREAD

A quick and easy strawberry spread that can be used as a jam or a syrup. Make extra during strawberry season and freeze it for later use.

2	.env	unflavored gelatin
1	C	frozen unsweetened apple juice concentrate, thawed
2	qts	fresh strawberries, washed, hulled, and mashed
1	T	lemon juice

1. Sprinkle gelatin over 1/2 cup apple juice concentrate; set aside.

2. Combine remaining 1/2 cup apple juice concentrate, strawberries, and lemon juice in heavy saucepan. Cook over medium-low heat 10 to 15 minutes, stirring constantly.

3. Remove from heat and add softened gelatin mixture; stir until gelatin dissolves. Cool and store in refrigerator.

Yield: 6 cups or 96 (1-tablespoon) servings

	RCU	FU	Cal	%Fat	P	F	C	Na
Per Tablespoon	0	0	9	0	T	T	2	1

4 Tablespoons = 1/2 Fruit exchange

APRICOT SPREAD

Great-tasting as a syrup on pancakes or waffles or as a jam on toast. Make extra during apricot season and freeze it for later.

3	C	apricot puree
1	pkg	Certo
1	C	frozen unsweetened pineapple-orange concentrate, thawed
1	8-oz can	crushed pineapple, drained

1. Cook fruit puree and bring to a boil; boil for 2 minutes.

2. Add juice concentrate and crushed pineapple; bring mixture to a full rolling boil.

3. Add Certo and cook 1 minute longer.

4. Freeze extra apricot spread for later use.

Yield: 2 1/2 pints

	RCU	FU	Cal	%Fat	P	F	C	Na
Per Tablespoon	0	0	16	T	.2	T	4	T

4 Tablespoons = 1 Fruit exchange

APPLE-STRAWBERRY JAM

A great-tasting jam--you'll love it on toast.

2	lb	strawberries, hulled and quartered
1	med	Red Delicious apple, peeled, cored, and finely chopped
¼	C	frozen unsweetened pineapple juice concentrate, thawed
¼	C	frozen unsweetened apple juice concentrate, thawed

1. Combine strawberries, apple, and pineapple juice concentrate in a large heavy saucepan; stir well. Let stand for 30 minutes.

2. Bring to a boil; cook over medium heat 15 minutes, stirring frequently. Continue to boil until candy thermometer registers 220°.

3. Remove mixture from the heat and skim off foam with a metal spoon.

4. Quickly pour jam into hot jars, leaving 1/4-inch headspace; cover at once with metal lids, and screw on bands. Process in boiling-water bath 10 minutes or keep jam refrigerated.

Yield: 3 cups or 48 1-tablespoon servings

	RCU	FU	Cal	%Fat	P	F	C	Na
Per Tablespoon	0	0	12	6	T	T	3	1

3 Tablespoons = 1/2 Fruit exchange

RASPBERRY APPLE JAM

Whenever you have raspberries, a delicious jam follows.

1	lb	Golden Delicious apples, cored and diced
6	T	frozen unsweetened apple juice concentrate, thawed
6	T	water
2	T	frozen unsweetened pineapple juice concentrate, thawed
¾	C	chopped dried apples
1	lb	fresh raspberries

1. Combine fresh apples, apple juice concentrate, water, and pineapple juice concentrate in heavy saucepan. Cover and cook over low heat 15 minutes.

2. Add dried apples and cook, uncovered, for 5 minutes.

3. Stir in raspberries; cover and cook over low heat for 5 minutes.

4. Remove cover and cook over medium heat for 10 to 15 minutes or until thickened, stirring frequently.

5. Quickly pour jam into hot jars, leaving 1/4-inch headspace; cover at once with metal lids, and screw on bands. Process in boiling-water bath 10 minutes or keep jam refrigerated.

Yield: 3 cups or 48 (1-tablespoon) servings

	RCU	FU	Cal	%Fat	P	F	C	Na
Per Tablespoon	0	0	18	5	T	T	5	2

2 Tablespoons = 1/2 Fruit exchange

KIWI PEAR JAM

This jam looks unusual but has a great taste.

1	lb	kiwifruit, peeled and chopped
½	lb	Golden Delicious apples, peeled, cored, and chopped
¾	C	chopped dried pears (12-14 pear halves)
¼	C	frozen unsweetened orange juice concentrate, thawed
1	tsp	grated orange peel

1. Combine all ingredients in a heavy saucepan. Cover and cook over low heat 20 minutes.

2. Increase heat to medium; cook, uncovered, 20 minutes or until thick, stirring frequently.

3. Quickly pour jam into hot jars, leaving 1/4-inch headspace. Cover at once with metal lids, and screw on bands. Process in boiling-water bath 10 minutes.

Yield: 2 cups or 32 (1-tablespoon) servings

	RCU	FU	Cal	%Fat	P	F	C	Na
Per Tablespoon	0	0	24	4	T	T	6	1

3 Tablespoons = 1 Fruit exchange

APPLE BUTTER

In Tennessee, we watched great vats of apple butter being prepared. Just the aroma was enough to make you want to indulge! This is an easy version of the famous spicy apple butters. It is great used like a jam on biscuits or toast or as a topping for pancakes or waffles.

1		24-oz unsweetened applesauce bottle
¾	C	frozen unsweetened apple juice concentrate, thawed
1	tsp	cinnamon
¼	tsp	nutmeg
¼	tsp	ground cloves

1. Combine all ingredients in a saucepan. Simmer, stirring occasionally, for about 2 hours, or until thick.

Yield: 2 cups or 32 (1-tablespoon) servings

	RCU	FU	Cal	%Fat	P	F	C	Na
Per Tablespoon	0	0	20	2	T	T	5	2

3 Tablespoons = 1 Fruit exchange

FRUIT PANCAKE TOPPING

Very tasty pancake topping.

2	C	unsweetened applesauce
½	C	unsweetened crushed pineapple, drained
½	tsp	cinnamon
1	C	plain nonfat yogurt

1. Combine applesauce, pineapple, and cinnamon in a bowl. Chill.

2. Just before serving, add yogurt.

3. Serve on pancakes, waffles, french toast, and so on.

Yield: 3 1/2 cups topping or 14 (1/4-cup) servings

	RCU	FU	Cal	%Fat	P	F	C	Na
Per Serving	0	0	30	1.7	1	T	7	13

1 Serving = 1/3 Fruit exchange

STRAWBERRY SYRUP

A delicious syrup for pancakes or waffles.

1	C	mashed strawberries
⅓	C	frozen unsweetened apple juice concentrate, thawed
1	T	quick-cooking tapioca

1. Combine ingredients in a blender; blend until smooth.

2. Pour into a saucepan; bring to a boil, stirring constantly.

3. Remove from heat and serve warm.

Yield: 4 (1/3-cup) servings

	RCU	FU	Cal	%Fat	P	F	C	Na
Per Serving	0	0	68	5	T	T	17	7

1 Serving = 1 Fruit exchange

PEACH SYRUP

Great fruit syrup for pancakes, waffles, or French toast. Take advantage of fresh peaches during the summer, and use frozen peaches during the rest of the year.

2	C	pureed peaches
1	T	lemon juice
2	T	cornstarch
¾	C	frozen unsweetened apple juice concentrate, thawed

1. Place all ingredients into blender container; blend until smooth.

2. Cook over medium heat until thickened, stirring constantly.

3. Serve warm or cold over pancakes or waffles.

4. Refrigerate extra syrup.

Yield: 11 (1/4-cup) servings

	RCU	FU	Cal	%Fat	P	F	C	Na
Per Serving	0	0	51	2	T	T	13	5

1 Serving = 1 Fruit exchange

APPLE SYRUP

This recipe is a quick, easy, and delicious syrup for pancakes or waffles.

| 1½ | C | frozen unsweetened apple juice concentrate, thawed |
| 1 | T | cornstarch |

1. Whisk cornstarch into cold apple juice concentrate until the cornstarch is dissolved. Heat to boiling over medium heat, stirring constantly.

2. Serve warm over pancakes or waffles.

Yield: 6 (1/4-cup) servings

	RCU	FU	Cal	%Fat	P	F	C	Na
Per Serving	0	0	122	2	0	0	30	18

1 Serving = 2 Fruit exchange

CITRUS FRUIT SAUCE

Great served hot over pancakes and waffles; for a taste-tempting change of pace, chill it for a great fresh fruit sauce.

1½	C	frozen unsweetened orange juice, thawed
¼	C	frozen unsweetened apple juice concentrate, thawed
¼	C	water
2	T	cornstarch
¼	tsp	lemon juice

1. Whisk cornstarch into orange juice, apple juice concentrate, and water.

2. Cook over medium heat until thickened, stirring constantly.

3. Remove from heat and add lemon juice.

4. Serve hot over pancakes and waffles or chilled as a sauce for fresh fruit.

5. Store in refrigerator.

Yield: 4 cups or 16 (1/4-cup) servings

	RCU	FU	Cal	%Fat	P	F	C	Na
Per Serving	0	0	29	1	0	0	7	2

1 Serving = 1/2 Fruit exchange

FRESH FRUIT SAUCE

Try this recipe over pancakes and waffles--or, for a change of pace, mix it with plain non-fat yogurt.

2	C	sliced fresh strawberries OR
		raspberries OR
		sliced peaches
2	T	cornstarch
½	C	frozen unsweetened apple juice concentrate, thawed

1. Whisk cornstarch into apple juice concentrate; bring to a boil.

2. Add 1 cup fruit, and bring to a boil again.

3. Remove from heat; add remaining fruit (don't cook any further).

4. Serve hot or cold.

Yield: 2 1/2 cups or 10 (1/4-cup) servings

	RCU	FU	Cal	%Fat	P	F	C	Na
Per Serving	0	0	38	4	T	T	9	4

1 Serving = 1/2 Fruit exchange

Chapter Ten

Muffins & Breads

Muffins & Breads

Nothin' says lovin' like muffins and breads! Muffins are becoming increasingly popular--there are even shops that specialize in muffins alone. You might remember muffins as being yeast-free, bread-like goodies that were eaten with butter or jam because they weren't sweet enough. Today's muffins are a different story: they're more like cupcakes than bread!

This chapter gives muffins a new meaning. Not only are they sweet, but they are made without any added oil or fat. You can safely eat these muffins, even if you are trying to lose weight. Muffins are great as part of breakfast, lunch, or dinner-- and you'll find that muffins are also excellent snacks, especially for people with hypoglycemia.

Muffins are easy to make, and even children enjoy preparing them. Save time in the kitchen by making extra and freezing them.

Quick breads are usually notoriously high in sugar and fat (up to 52 percent and higher), but the breads in this chapter are nutritious, low in sugars, and low in fat. They are quick and easy to make and delicious served with breakfast or for a snack or dessert. Over-ripe bananas take on a new meaning once you make one of the banana breads listed in this chapter. You'll actually look forward to finding a few overripe bananas on the counter!

The recipe for sweet rolls lets you keep cinnamon roll-like items around. This is the only recipe that has a small amount of salt in it. (Salt is a yeast inhibitor and improves bread texture.) The fruit fillings are especially delicious in the sweet rolls. For a really fancy treat, try the Swedish Tea Ring.

Picture: Fruitcake, p. 46.

PINEAPPLE CARROT MUFFINS

This moist, full-flavored muffin is an all-time favorite of everyone who tastes it.

2	C	whole wheat flour
¼	C	wheat germ
1½	tsp	baking soda
¼	C	frozen unsweetened apple juice concentrate, thawed
¾	C	frozen unsweetened pineapple juice concentrate, thawed
2	lg	egg whites
1	tsp	vanilla
½	C	unsweetened crushed pineapple, drained
1	C	finely grated carrots

1. Combine flour, wheat germ, and soda.

2. Combine juice concentrates, egg whites, vanilla, pineapple, and carrots; add to the dry ingredients. Stir until just moistened.

3. Spray muffin tin with nonstick vegetable coating. Pour batter into muffin tin. Bake at 400° for 15 to 20 minutes.

Yield: 12 muffins

	RCU	FU	Cal	%Fat	P	F	C	Na
Per Muffin	0	0	119	4	4	T	27	117

1 Muffin = 1/2 Fruit; 1 Bread exchange

Pictured: Banana Waffles, p. 141; Strawberry Spread, 149; Banana Cream, p. 195; Peach Syrup, p. 156; Pineapple Carrot Muffins, p. 161.

APPLE OATMEAL MUFFINS

A repeatedly requested favorite of all who have eaten it.

1¼	C	whole wheat flour
1	C	quick-cooking rolled oats
2	tsp	baking powder
1	tsp	baking soda
1½	tsp	cinnamon
2	lg	egg whites
1	C	frozen unsweetened apple juice concentrate, thawed
2	C	chopped apples

1. Combine flour, oats, baking powder, baking soda, and cinnamon.

2. In separate bowl, combine egg whites, apple juice concentrate, and chopped apples.

3. Add liquid mixture to dry ingredients; blend until just moistened.

4. Divide batter into 12 muffin tins that have been sprayed with nonstick vegetable coating.

5. Bake at 350° for 20 to 25 minutes.

Yield: 12 muffins

	RCU	FU	Cal	%Fat	P	F	C	Na
Per Muffin	0	0	129	T	3	T	28	135

1 Muffin = 1 Fruit exchange; 1 Bread exchange

APPLE CARROT MUFFINS

A tasty muffin that will be sure to delight!

½	C	skim milk
¾	C	frozen unsweetened apple juice concentrate, thawed
3	lg	egg whites
1	tsp	vanilla
2½	C	whole wheat flour
3	tsp	baking powder
¼	tsp	nutmeg
1	tsp	cinnamon
1	C	grated apple, peeled and cored
1	C	finely grated carrot
1	C	chopped nuts, optional

1. Combine milk, apple juice concentrate, egg whites, and vanilla; beat well.

2. In separate bowl, combine flour, baking powder, nutmeg, and cinnamon.

3. Add milk mixture to flour mixture; blend until just moistened. Stir in apple, carrot, and nuts.

4. Spray muffin tins with nonstick vegetable coating. Fill tins three-fourths full.

5. Bake at 400° for 15 to 20 minutes.

Yield: 18 muffins

	RCU	FU	Cal	%Fat	P	F	C	Na
Per Muffin	0	0	87	4	3	0	19	67

1 Muffin = 1/2 Fruit exchange; 1 Bread exchange

APPLESAUCE OAT MUFFINS

You'll enjoy this at breakfast.

1½	C	unprocessed oat bran
1	C	quick-cooking rolled oats
1	T	baking powder
½	C	chunky or smooth unsweetened applesauce
2	lg	egg whites
½	C	skim milk
¾	C	frozen unsweetened apple juice concentrate, thawed
½	C	raisins

1. Combine dry ingredients; mix well.

2. Blend applesauce, egg whites, milk, and juice concentrate. Add to dry ingredients. Stir until just moistened.

3. Spray muffin cups with nonstick vegetable coating. Spoon batter into prepared muffin cups. Bake at 400° for 15 to 20 minutes, or until done.

Yield: 12 muffins

	RCU	FU	Cal	%Fat	P	F	C	Na
Per Muffin	0	0	124	5	4	1	25	95

1 Muffin = 1 Fruit exchange; 1 Bread exchange

APPLE BRAN MUFFINS

A hearty whole-grain muffin to accompany any meal.

½	C	unprocessed bran
½	C	untoasted wheat germ
1½	C	whole wheat flour
½	C	nonfat dry milk
3	tsp	baking powder
½	C	raisins
½	C	chopped walnuts, optional
2	lg	egg whites
1½	C	frozen unsweetened apple juice concentrate, thawed
1	T	cold-pressed oil

1. In a large bowl, combine bran, wheat germ, flour, dry milk, baking powder, raisins, and walnuts.

2. Beat to blend egg whites, apple juice concentrate, and oil. Add to dry ingredients and stir to mix well.

3. Spray muffin tin with nonstick vegetable coating. Spoon batter into muffin cups, filling to the top. Bake at 350° for 15 to 20 minutes.

Yield: 12 muffins

	RCU	FU	Cal	%Fat	P	F	C	Na
Per Muffin	0	0	172	12	6	2	35	112

1 Muffin = 1 Fruit exchange; 1 Bread exchange

APRICOT BRAN MUFFINS

An unusual combination that everyone enjoys.

2	C	unprocessed bran flakes
2	C	whole wheat flour
2	tsp	baking powder
½	tsp	baking soda
1	C	dried apricots, finely chopped
2	lg	egg whites
1	C	buttermilk
¾	C	frozen unsweetened pineapple-orange juice concentrate, thawed
1	tsp	vanilla

1. In large bowl, combine dry ingredients; mix well. Add apricots and toss lightly, making sure apricot pieces are evenly coated with flour mixture.

2. In small bowl, blend egg whites, buttermilk, juice concentrate, and vanilla. Add to dry ingredients. Stir until just moistened.

3. Spray muffin cups with nonstick vegetable coating. Spoon batter into prepared muffin cups. Bake at 400° for 15 to 20 minutes, or until done.

Yield: 12 muffins

	RCU	FU	Cal	%Fat	P	F	C	Na
Per Muffin	0	0	155	7	6	1	35	119

1 Muffin = 1 Fruit exchange; 1 Bread exchange

CRANBERRY-ORANGE MUFFINS

These muffins have a wonderfully tart taste, yet are plenty sweet. They are a great way to set off the holiday season.

2	C	whole wheat flour
1½	tsp	baking soda
1	tsp	grated orange rind
1	C	plain nonfat yogurt
1	lg	egg white
¼	C	frozen unsweetened pineapple-orange concentrate, thawed
½	C	frozen unsweetened apple juice concentrate, thawed
1	C	chopped cranberries

1. Combine flour, baking soda, and orange rind in large bowl.

2. Combine yogurt, egg white, and juices; add to dry ingredients, stirring just until moistened.

3. Fold in cranberries.

4. Spoon into muffin pan sprayed with nonstick vegetable coating.

5. Bake at 375° for 20 to 25 minutes.

Yield: 12 muffins

	RCU	FU	Cal	%Fat	P	F	C	Na
Per Muffin	0	0	110	4	4	T	24	125

1 Muffin = 1/2 Fruit exchange; 1 Bread exchange

BLUEBERRY MUFFINS

This great-tasting muffin is especially fun to make during fresh blueberry season.

1	C	whole wheat flour
1½	C	quick-cooking rolled oats
2	tsp	baking powder
½	tsp	baking soda
2	lg	egg whites
½	C	buttermilk
¾	C	frozen unsweetened pineapple-orange juice concentrate, thawed
1	tsp	vanilla
1	C	unsweetened fresh* blueberries

1. Combine flour, oats, baking powder, and baking soda.

2. In separate bowl, combine egg whites, buttermilk, juice concentrate, and vanilla.

3. Add liquid mixture to dry ingredients; blend until just moistened. Gently fold in blueberries.

4. Divide batter into 12 muffin tins that have been sprayed with nonstick vegetable coating.

5. Bake at 400° for 15 to 20 minutes.

Frozen blueberries may be used, but they make the batter a little more moist

Yield: 12 muffins

	RCU	FU	Cal	%Fat	P	F	C	Na
Per Muffin	0	0	114	8	4	1	23	107

1 Muffin = 1/2 Fruit exchange; 1 Bread exchange

BANANA OATMEAL RAISIN MUFFINS

A firm, good-tasting muffin that's sure to please your entire family.

1¼	C	whole wheat flour
¾	C	quick-cooking rolled oats
2	tsp	baking powder
¼	tsp	baking soda
¾	C	frozen unsweetened apple juice concentrate, thawed
1	lg	egg white
2	med	ripe bananas, mashed (1 cup)
¼	C	raisins

1. Combine flour, oats, baking powder, and baking soda.

2. Combine apple juice concentrate, egg white, and mashed bananas; add to the dry ingredients. Stir until just moistened.

3. Gently stir in raisins.

4. Spray muffin pan with nonstick vegetable coating. Pour batter into muffin tin. Bake at 400° for 15 minutes.

Yield: 12 muffins

	RCU	FU	Cal	%Fat	P	F	C	Na
Per Muffin	0	0	125	6	3	T	28	79

1 Muffin = 1 Fruit exchange; 1 Bread exchange

OATMEAL MUFFINS

This tasty muffin is great for breakfast, snacks, or as an accompaniment to a meal.

1	C	quick-cooking rolled oats
1	C	whole wheat flour
1	tsp	baking powder
½	tsp	baking soda
1	lg	egg white
½	tsp	vanilla
½	tsp	coconut extract
¼	C	frozen unsweetened pineapple juice concentrate, thawed
½	C	frozen unsweetened apple juice concentrate, thawed
½	C	unsweetened crushed pineapple, drained
½	C	buttermilk

1. Combine dry ingredients. Stir well.

2. Combine the remaining ingredients and add them to the dry ingredients. Stir until just moistened.

3. Spray muffin pans with nonstick vegetable coating fill muffin tins two-thirds full.

4. Bake at 400° for 15 to 20 minutes, or until brown.

Yield: 12 muffins

	RCU	FU	Cal	%Fat	P	F	C	Na
Per Muffin	0	0	103	7	3	T	21	79

1 Muffin = 1/2 Fruit exchange; 1 Bread exchange

SPICY PEAR MUFFINS

Great way to use fresh pears.

2	lg	egg whites
1	lg	pear, pureed (about 1 cup)
¼	C	unsweetened pineapple juice concentrate
½	C	unsweetened apple juice concentrate
1	C	quick cooking oats
1¼	C	whole wheat flour
½	tsp	nutmeg
½	tsp	cinnamon
1	tsp	baking soda
2	tsp	baking powder
½	C	chopped almonds, optional

1. Combine juices, egg whites, and pureed pears; add to dry ingredients, stirring just until moistened.

2. Combine dry ingredients in a large bowl.

3. Fold in chopped almonds.

4. Spoon into muffin pan sprayed with nonstick vegetable coating.

5. Bake at 375° for 15 to 20 minutes.

Yield: 12 muffins

	RCU	FU	Cal	%Fat	P	F	C	Na
Per Muffin	0	0	112	7	4	1	24	132

1 Muffin = 1/2 Fruit exchange; 1 Bread exchange

PEAR MUFFINS

This taste-tempting moist muffin is a great way to use fresh pears.

1	lg	egg white
1	C	finely chopped fresh pears
1	C	frozen unsweetened apple juice concentrate, thawed
2	C	whole wheat flour
1	tsp	baking soda
2	tsp	baking powder
½	tsp	nutmeg

1. Combine flour, baking soda, baking powder, and nutmeg in large bowl.

2. Combine apple juice concentrate and egg white; add to dry ingredients, stirring just until moistened.

3. Fold in chopped pears.

4. Spoon into muffin pan sprayed with nonstick vegetable coating.

5. Bake at 350° for 15 to 20 minutes.

Yield: 12 muffins

	RCU	FU	Cal	%Fat	P	F	C	Na
Per Muffin	0	0	125	5	3	T	28	131

1 Muffin = 1 Fruit exchange; 1 Bread exchange

PUMPKIN NUT MUFFINS

A spicy sweet pumpkin muffin, this is a great breakfast accompaniment or snack.

1¾	C	whole wheat flour
1	tsp	baking soda
½	tsp	baking powder
1	tsp	cinnamon
½	tsp	nutmeg
¼	tsp	ginger
2	lg	egg whites
⅓	C	buttermilk
½	tsp	vanilla extract
¾	C	frozen unsweetened apple juice concentrate, thawed
1	C	canned pumpkin
¼	C	chopped pecans, optional

1. Combine flour, baking soda, baking powder, cinnamon, nutmeg, and ginger.

2. Combine egg whites, buttermilk, vanilla, apple juice concentrate, and pumpkin; add to the dry ingredients. Stir until just moistened.

3. Fold in nuts.

4. Spray muffin tin with nonstick vegetable coating. Pour batter into muffin tin. Bake at 375° for 20 minutes.

Yield: 12 muffins

	RCU	FU	Cal	%Fat	P	F	C	Na
Per Muffin	0	0	102	5	3	T	22	103

1 Muffin = 1/2 Fruit exchange; 1 Bread exchange

PUMPKIN-RAISIN MUFFINS

A delicious, not-too-spicy muffin that is great for breakfast or snacks.

1¼	C	whole wheat flour
½	C	wheat germ
2	tsp	baking soda
¾	tsp	cinnamon
2	lg	egg whites
½	C	canned pumpkin
1	tsp	vanilla
¾	C	frozen unsweetened apple juice concentrate, thawed
¼	C	raisins

1.   Combine all dry ingredients.

2.   Combine egg whites, pumpkin, vanilla, and apple juice concentrate; add to the dry ingredients until just moistened.

3.   Fold in raisins.

4.   Spray muffin tin with nonstick vegetable coating. Bake at 375° for 15 to 20 minutes.

Yield: 12 muffins

	RCU	FU	Cal	%Fat	P	F	C	Na
Per Muffin	0	0	103	7	4	T	22	151

1 Muffin = 1/2 Fruit; 1 Bread

DATE OAT BRAN MUFFINS

Oat bran muffins are especially important for those who are battling high cholesterol. This muffin not only tastes good, but is good for you.

2⅓	C	oat bran
2	tsp	baking soda
½	C	mashed bananas
2	lg	egg whites
¼	C	frozen unsweetened apple juice concentrate, thawed
½	C	frozen unsweetened pineapple-orange-banana concentrate, thawed
½	C	skim milk
⅓	C	chopped dates
¼	C	chopped walnuts, optional

1. Combine oat bran and baking soda in a large bowl.

2. Combine mashed bananas, egg whites, juice concentrates, and skim milk. Add to oat bran mixture.

3. Stir in dates and nuts.

4. Spray muffin tin with nonstick vegetable coating and divide batter among the 12 muffin cups. Bake at 375° for 15 to 20 minutes.

Yield: 12 muffins

	RCU	FU	Cal	%Fat	P	F	C	Na
Per Muffin	0	0	133	9	4	1	27	153

1 Muffin = 1 Fruit exchange; 1 Bread exchange

APPLESAUCE OAT BRAN MUFFINS

Great accompaniment to any breakfast. Two oat bran muffins per day appears to assist in lowering cholesterol.

2¼	C	oat bran
1	T	baking powder
½	C	unsweetened applesauce
¾	C	frozen unsweetened apple juice concentrate, thawed
½	C	skim milk
2	lg	egg whites
½	C	raisins

1. Mix oat bran and baking powder together in a large bowl.

2. Combine applesauce, thawed apple juice concentrate, milk, and egg whites; add to oat bran mixture. Stir until combined. Add raisins.

3. Spray muffin tin with nonstick vegetable coating. Divide batter among the 12 muffin cups. Bake at 375° for 15 to 20 minutes.

Yield: 12 muffins

	RCU	FU	Cal	%Fat	P	F	C	Na
Per Muffin	0	0	118	28	4	1	24	98

1 Muffin = 1 Fruit exchange; 1 Bread exchange

OAT BRAN PRUNE MUFFINS

A hearty whole-grain muffin doesn't taste like it contains prunes! Oat bran has been shown to be beneficial in lowering cholesterol.

2¼	C	oat bran
2	tsp	baking powder
½	tsp	baking soda
½	C	skim milk
2	lg	egg whites
½	C	unsweetened applesauce
½	C	frozen unsweetened orange juice concentrate, thawed
¼	C	frozen unsweetened apple juice concentrate, thawed
⅔	C	finely chopped pitted prunes

1. Combine dry ingredients in a bowl.

2. Combine milk, egg whites, applesauce, and juice concentrates; add to dry ingredients, stirring until just combined.

3. Fold in chopped prunes.

4. Pour into 12 muffin cups that have been sprayed with nonstick vegetable coating.

5. Bake at 350° for 15 to 20 minutes.

Yield: 12 muffins

	RCU	FU	Cal	%Fat	P	F	C	Na
Per Muffin	0	0	124	8	4	1	26	103

1 Muffin = 1 Fruit exchange; 1 Bread exchange

BANANA BREAD

This moist, sweet bread--a great way to use overripe bananas--will become a certain favorite. Best of all, you'll never miss the sugar in this one!

3	med	ripe bananas
1 2	lg	egg white
¾	C	frozen unsweetened apple juice concentrate, thawed ¼ + c. Fruit Sweet
¼	C	margarine or butter, melted or ⅓ c. oil
2¼	C	whole wheat flour— berries ½ tsp. cinnamon
1	tsp	baking soda + 1½ tsp. baking powder ½ tsp. grated orange peel
½—1	C	chopped walnuts, optional
½	C	currents (softened in boiling water)

1. Mash bananas. Mix in egg white, apple juice concentrate, and melted butter.

2. Add flour and baking soda. Mix well.

3. Stir in walnuts.

4. Pour into an 8 1/2" x 4 1/2" loaf pan that has been sprayed with nonstick vegetable coating.

5. Bake at 325° for 45 to 50 minutes. Leave in pan for 10 minutes and remove; cool. Wrap in plastic wrap or plastic bag overnight so the banana flavor will develop.

Variation: Banana Poppy Seed Bread

1. Instead of walnuts, stir in 1/4 cup poppy seeds.

Yield: 16 slices

	RCU	FU	Cal	%Fat	P	F	C	Na
Per Slice	0	0	131	23	3	3	24	92

1 Slice = 1 Fruit exchange; 1/2 Bread exchange; 1/2 Fat exchange

BANANA ORANGE BREAD

A very nice sweet bread. This would make a nice accompaniment to a breakfast or brunch.

1¼	C	whole wheat flour
1	C	quick-cooking rolled oats
1	T	baking powder
½	tsp	baking soda
⅔	C	mashed ripe banana (about 2 medium)
½	C	frozen unsweetened pineapple-orange-banana concentrate, thawed
¼	C	margarine or butter, melted
1	lg	egg white
½	tsp	grated orange peel

1. Spray 8 1/2" x 4 1/2" loaf pan with nonstick vegetable coating.

2. Mix banana, juice concentrate, butter, egg white, and orange peel until well combined.

3. Add flour, oats, baking powder, and baking soda; mix until well blended.

4. Pour into prepared pan. Bake at 325° for 45 minutes.

5. Cool 10 minutes and remove from pan. When completely cool, wrap in a plastic bag overnight. The full banana flavor develops when stored overnight.

Yield: 16 slices

	RCU	FU	Cal	%Fat	P	F	C	Na
Per Slice	0	0	112	28	3	4	19	121

1 Slice = 1/2 Fruit exchange; 1/2 Bread exchange; 1/2 Fat exchange

BANANA-APPLESAUCE BREAD

A nice, moist, mildly flavored banana nut bread.

2¼	C	whole wheat flour
1	tsp	baking soda
2	lg	egg whites
½	C	mashed banana (1 medium)
½	C	unsweetened applesauce
¾	C	frozen unsweetened apple juice concentrate, thawed
¼	C	cold-pressed oil
¼	C	raisins
¼	C	chopped walnuts, optional

1. Beat egg whites until frothy. Add mashed banana, applesauce, apple juice concentrate, and oil; beat well.

2. Add flour and baking soda. Beat until smooth.

3. Fold in raisins and walnuts.

4. Spray an 8 1/2" x 4 1/2" loaf pan with nonstick vegetable coating. Pour batter into prepared pan. Bake at 325° for 50 to 60 minutes or until a toothpick inserted in center comes out clean.

5. Let sit in pan for 10 minutes; remove and cool on a rack.

Yield: 16 slices

	RCU	FU	Cal	%Fat	P	F	C	Na
Per Slice	0	0	129	27	3	4	22	62

1 Slice = 1/2 Fruit exchange; 1/2 Bread exchange; 1/2 Fat exchange

BANANA BLUEBERRY BREAD

Blueberry lovers will be sure to enjoy this recipe. The banana flavor develops fully if stored overnight in a plastic container.

1	C	mashed bananas (about 2 medium)
2	lg	egg whites
¾	C	frozen unsweetened apple juice concentrate, thawed
2	C	whole wheat flour
½	C	rolled oats, quick-cooking or regular
2	tsp	baking powder
½	tsp	baking soda
¼	C	margarine or butter, melted
½	C	unsweetened fresh or frozen blueberries

or ⅓ c. apple + ¼ c. raspberry

1. Beat bananas until smooth. Add egg whites and beat until frothy. Add apple juice concentrate and mix well.

2. Add flour, oats, baking powder, and baking soda; mix until smooth.

3. Add melted butter and beat until well combined.

4. Gently fold in blueberries.

5. Spray an 8 1/2" x 4 1/2" loaf pan with nonstick vegetable coating. Pour batter into prepared pan.

6. Bake at 325° for 60 minutes or until a wooden toothpick comes out clean when inserted into the center of the loaf.

7. Let sit in pan for 10 minutes. Remove from pan and cool on a rack.

Yield: 16 slices

	RCU	FU	Cal	%Fat	P	F	C	Na
Per Slice	0	0	130	24	3	4	23	108

1 Slice = 1/2 Fruit exchange; 1 Bread exchange; 1/2 Fat exchange

DATE NUT BREAD

A delicious easy-to-make nut bread to eat as a dessert or snack.

1	C	cut-up pitted dates
1	tsp	baking soda
¾	C	frozen unsweetened apple juice concentrate, thawed
¼	C	water
2	T	margarine or butter, melted
2	lg	egg whites
1¾	C	whole wheat flour
½	C	chopped walnuts, optional

1. Sprinkle baking soda over dates. Combine water and apple juice concentrate and bring to a boil. Pour the boiling liquid over the date and soda mixture.

2. Beat egg whites until fluffy. Add date mixture and mix.

3. Add flour, melted butter, and nuts. Mix well.

4. Spray an 8 1/2" x 4 1/2" loaf pan with nonstick vegetable coating. Pour batter into prepared loaf pan.

5. Bake at 300° for 1 hour.

Yield: 16 slices

	RCU	FU	Cal	%Fat	P	F	C	Na
Per Slice	0	0	111	15	3	2	23	78

1 Slice = 1 Fruit exchange; 1/2 Bread exchange

ORANGE-DATE NUT LOAF

A delicious mildly orange-flavored nut bread. A slightly different flavor for a date bread.

1½	C	whole wheat flour
1	tsp	baking powder
½	tsp	baking soda
1	tsp	grated orange rind
¾	C	chopped and pitted moist dates
2	lg	egg whites
¼	C	frozen unsweetened orange juice concentrate, thawed
½	C	frozen unsweetened apple juice concentrate, thawed
3	T	margarine or butter, melted
½	C	chopped pecans, optional

1. Beat egg whites until frothy. Add orange and apple juice concentrates.
    Blend. Add dates.

2. Combine flour, baking powder, and baking soda; add to date mixture. Mix
    until well combined.

3. Add melted butter, orange rind, and pecans.

4. Spray an 8 1/2" x 4 1/2" loaf pan with vegetable coating. Pour batter into
    prepared pan. Bake at 325° for 45 minutes.

5. Cool in pan for 10 minutes. Remove from pan; cool on rack.

Yield: 16 slices

	RCU	FU	Cal	%Fat	P	F	C	Na
Per Slice	0	0	102	21	2	2	19	79

1 Slice = 1 Fruit exchange; 1/2 Bread exchange; 1/2 Fat exchange

PUMPKIN OATMEAL BREAD

A moist sweet bread that can be used as a dessert, a snack, or an accompaniment to any breakfast. This is pictured on the cover.

½	C	raisins *Currents*
¼	C	margarine or butter, softened *oil*
2	lg	egg whites *eggs*
¾	C	frozen unsweetened apple juice concentrate, thawed *or apple-rasp (½c) + Fruit Sweet (¼c)*
1	C	canned pumpkin
1	C	whole wheat flour *≡ 1 c. wheat berries*
1	C	rolled oats
¼	tsp	baking powder
1	tsp	baking soda
¾	tsp	cinnamon
⅛	tsp	ground cloves
¼	tsp	nutmeg *or pecans*
⅓	C	chopped walnuts, optional

1. Soak raisins in hot water; set aside.

2. Cream softened butter and egg whites; add juice concentrate.

3. Blend in canned pumpkin.

4. Add flour, oats, baking powder, baking soda, cinnamon, cloves, and nutmeg; beat until smooth.

5. Drain water from raisins.

6. Fold in raisins and nuts.

7. Pour into a 9" x 5" loaf pan that has been sprayed with nonstick vegetable coating.

8. *For a decorative touch:* you may sprinkle whole rolled oats over top before baking.

9. Bake at 325° for 1 hour, or until done.

        350°   + 10'

Yield: 18 slices

	RCU	FU	Cal	%Fat	P	F	C	Na
Per Slice	0	0	101	27.6	2	3	17	86

1 Slice = 1/2 Fruit exchange; 1/2 Bread exchange; 1/2 Fat exchange

SPICED APPLESAUCE BREAD

A spicy sweet bread you will love! Everyone else did too.

1¾	C	whole wheat flour
1	tsp	baking soda
½	tsp	baking powder
½	tsp	cinnamon
¼	tsp	nutmeg
¼	tsp	allspice
1	C	finely chopped apple, peeled and cored
¾	C	frozen unsweetened apple juice concentrate, thawed
¼	C	unsweetened applesauce
¼	C	cold-pressed oil
2	lg	egg whites
⅓	C	chopped walnuts, optional

1. Combine first 6 ingredients and set aside. Mix apple, apple juice concentrate, applesauce, oil, and egg whites. Add to dry ingredients and mix well.

2. Spray an 8 1/2" x 4 1/2" loaf pan with nonstick vegetable coating. Pour batter into prepared pan.

3. Bake at 350° for 1 hour or until a toothpick inserted into center comes out clean. (It may need 5 to 10 minutes more baking time.)

4. Cool for 5 minutes in pan; remove and cool.

Yield: 16 slices

	RCU	FU	Cal	%Fat	P	F	C	Na
Per Slice	0	0	107	32	2	4	17	46

1 Slice = 1/2 Fruit exchange; 1/2 Bread exchange; 1/2 Fat exchange

STRAWBERRY NUT BREAD

Good served both warm or cold, this bread will be a nice accompaniment to your breakfast. Not as sweet as other nut breads.

1	C	strawberries, pureed (approximately 3/4 pint)
2	lg	egg whites
¾	C	frozen unsweetened apple juice concentrate, thawed
1¾	C	whole wheat flour
1	tsp	baking soda
¼	tsp	baking powder
½	tsp	cinnamon
¼	C	margarine or butter, melted
⅓	C	chopped walnuts or pecans, optional

1. Puree approximately 3/4 pint strawberries in blender to yield 1 cup. Pour pureed strawberries into small saucepan. Heat to boiling and cook for 1 minute, stirring constantly. Cool.

2. Beat egg whites until fluffy. Add apple juice concentrate, and blend. Add flour, soda, baking powder, and cinnamon; beat until smooth.

3. Add melted butter and cooked strawberries; blend until smooth. Fold in chopped nuts. Pour batter into an 8 1/2" x 4 1/2" loaf pan that has been sprayed with nonstick vegetable coating.

4. Bake at 325° for 1 hour or until done. Cool in pan for 5 minutes and remove from pan; cool on a wire rack.

5. When cool, wrap in plastic wrap. This bread is better when eaten the next day.

Yield: 16 slices

	RCU	FU	Cal	%Fat	P	F	C	Na
Per Slice	0	0	98	30	2	3	16	99

1 Slice = 1/2 Fruit exchange; 1/2 Bread exchange; 1/2 Fat exchange

SWEET ROLLS

At last, a cinnamon roll recipe that is not only tender and delicious, but also good for you! Try it with the different fruit fillings.

2	pkg	dry yeast
1	C	lukewarm water
1	C	skim milk, scalded
¼	C	margarine or butter, melted
½	C	honey
½	tsp	salt
1	lg	egg white
1	lg	egg, beaten
4	C	whole wheat flour
2 to		
2½	C	unbleached flour

1. Dissolve yeast in lukewarm water; set aside.

2. Scald milk; add butter, honey, and salt; cool to lukewarm.

3. Add 2 cups whole wheat flour to make a soft batter. Add yeast and beaten egg and egg white; beat well.

4. Add remaining flour, or enough to make a soft dough. Knead lightly and place in a greased bowl. Cover and set in a warm place. Let rise until double in bulk, about 2 hours.

5. Divide dough into 2 parts. Roll out half the dough to 1/4-inch thickness in a rectangular shape.

6. Spread with any of the following fillings. Roll up tightly, beginning at wide side. Seal well by pinching edges of roll together. Slice 3/4-inch thick and arrange on a cookie sheet sprayed with nonstick vegetable coating. Repeat with remaining dough.

7. Let rise 30 minutes. Bake 15 to 20 minutes at 375°.

Yield: 24 to 30 rolls or 2 Swedish Tea Rings

	RCU	FU	Cal	%Fat	P	F	C	Na
Per Roll	0	0	119	16	4	2	22	64

2 Rolls = 1/2 Fruit exchange; 2 Bread exchange; 1/2 Fat exchange

SWEDISH TEA RING

Use the Sweet Rolls recipe and proceed as follows:

1. Choose one of the fillings. Roll out 1/2 of the dough into a rectangle. Spread with filling.

2. Roll as for a jelly roll (rolling up on the length of the dough) and form into a ring (seam side down).

3. Place on a cookie sheet that has been sprayed with nonstick vegetable coating.

4. With scissors or a sharp serrated knife, make about 12 evenly divided cuts from the outer edge toward the center, halfway through. Twist the little cut half-slices upward so that the filling shows.

5. Bake at 350° for 20 to 30 minutes or until golden brown. To avoid excessive browning on top, slip a sheet of aluminum foil over the ring during the last half of the baking time.

Yield: 2 Swedish Tea Rings

RAISIN FILLING

1	C	raisins
½	tsp	cornstarch
½	C	frozen unsweetened apple juice concentrate, thawed
½	C	chopped nuts (walnuts, pecans, or almonds), optional
½	tsp	cinnamon
1	T	lemon juice

1. Combine raisins, cornstarch, juice concentrate, and nuts; cook, stirring constantly, 3 to 5 minutes, or until mixture reaches a spreading consistency.

2. Remove from heat and add lemon juice. Stir well and cool.

Yield: Filling for 1 small Swedish Tea Ring

	RCU	FU	Cal	%Fat	P	F	C	Na
Per Serving	0	0	23	2	T	T	6	2

1 Serving = 1/2 Fruit exchange

DATE FILLING

1	C	chopped dates
½	C	frozen unsweetened apple juice concentrate, thawed
½	C	chopped nuts (walnuts, pecans, or almonds), optional

1. Combine all ingredients in a small saucepan; cook, stirring constantly, until mixture reaches a spreading consistency.

Yield: Filling for 24 to 30 rolls or 1 small Swedish Tea Ring

	RCU	FU	Cal	%Fat	P	F	C	Na
Per Serving	0	0	24	2	T	T	6	1

1 Serving = 1/2 Fruit exchange

DRIED APRICOT FILLING

2	C	finely chopped dried apricots
½	C	frozen unsweetened pineapple juice concentrate, thawed
1	C	frozen unsweetened apple juice concentrate, thawed
1	tsp	lemon juice
½	C	chopped nuts (walnuts, pecans, or almonds), optional

1. Combine all ingredients in a small skillet or saucepan. Cook down until tender and thickened, stirring occasionally.

Yield: Filling for 24 to 30 rolls

	RCU	FU	Cal	%Fat	P	F	C	Na
Per Serving	0	0	39	2	T	T	10	3

1 Serving = 1/2 Fruit exchange

APPLE FILLING

1	lg	apple, peeled and cored
1	C	unsweetened applesauce
¾	C	frozen unsweetened apple juice concentrate, thawed
½	tsp	cinnamon
⅛	tsp	allspice

1. Grate apple. Place all ingredients in a saucepan and cook down until thickened; stir occasionally.

Yield: Filling for 12 to 15 rolls (1/2 the Sweet Rolls recipe)

	RCU	FU	Cal	%Fat	P	F	C	Na
Per Serving	0	0	38	3	T	T	10	4

1 Serving = 1/2 Fruit exchange

Chapter Eleven

Snacks & Treats

Snacks & Treats

Ready for a real potpourri? In this chapter you'll find simple recipes for delicious snacks and treats that didn't fall under the headings of the previous ten chapters. Make sure you look at the fat percentage in each recipe: some of the offerings in this chapter are intended for nutritious after-school snacks, and aren't suitable for weight control. Why? They contain peanut butter--a great source of protein and a healthy vegetable oil, but high in fat content.

You'll find a variety of ideas for canning fruits without sugar, and Geniel's Salsa is one of the best I've eaten. Try the salsa and homemade tortilla chips for a winning after-school snack.

Read through the recipes, and let your imagination soar. You--as well as your children--will love the variety of healthy, nutritious snacks and treats available to you!

BANANA CREAM

This is wonderful served like whipped topping--and without fat, too! Use on poached apples, pancakes, waffles, and anything else as a creamy topping.

1	lg	egg white, room temperature
1	T	frozen unsweetened apple juice concentrate, thawed
1	lg	ripe banana (1/2 cup)
1	T	lemon juice

1. Immediately before serving, beat 1 egg white until frothy in a small bowl. Gradually add apple juice concentrate, beating until well combined.

2. Mash large banana to make 1/2 cup; stir in lemon juice; add to egg white mixture. Beat to stiff peaks. Serve immediately.

Yield: 2 cups whipped topping or 8 (1/4-cup) servings

	RCU	FU	Cal	%Fat	P	F	C	Na
Per Serving	0	0	32	4	.7	T	8	8

1 Serving = 1/2 Fruit exchange

BANANA BITES

Bananas
Pineapple juice, unsweetened
Toasted wheat germ or finely chopped nuts

1.   Cut bananas into 1/2-inch pieces. Dip banana pieces into pineapple juice; roll in toasted wheat germ.

3.   Place on a cookie sheet and freeze. Store in plastic bags. Eat frozen.

Yield: About 5 pieces per each banana used

	RCU	FU	Cal	%Fat	P	F	C	Na
Per Banana	0	0	123	8	3	1	29	1

1 Banana = 1 1/2 Fruit exchange

JUICE POPSICLES

Fill popsicle trays or ice cube trays with any of the following unsweetened fruit juices and freeze:

1.   Orange
2.   Apple
3.   Pineapple
4.   Grape

Children can even have these for breakfast!

Yield: 1 6-oz can juice yields 12 1/4-cup servings

	RCU	FU	Cal	%Fat	P	F	C	Na
Per Serving	0	0	28	1	T	T	7	T

1 Serving = 1/2 Fruit exchange

FROZEN YOGURT SQUARES

The neighborhood children liked this one.

1	C	plain nonfat yogurt
⅓	C	unsweetened crushed pineapple, drained
1	tsp	vanilla
2	T	frozen unsweetened apple juice concentrate, thawed
1	C	sliced bananas
1	C	sliced strawberries
1	C	Grape Nuts

1. Place yogurt, pineapple, vanilla, juice concentrate, and bananas in blender container. Blend until smooth.

2. Place mixture in bowl; fold in sliced strawberries and 1/2 cup Grape Nuts cereal.

3. Pour into an 8" x 8" pan. Sprinkle remaining 1/2 cup Grape Nuts cereal evenly on top. Gently press cereal down.

4. Freeze. When ready to eat, let pan sit at room temperature for about 1/2 hour; cut into squares.

Yield: 36 squares

	RCU	FU	Cal	%Fat	P	F	C	Na
Per Square	0	0	27	3	1	T	6	27

2 Squares = 1/2 Fruit exchange

DANA DELIGHT

This is a nutritious snack that requires no baking. Just mix it up and store it in plastic wrap. This is a great snack for those who like back-packing or exploring the great outdoors--and it makes a good after-school snack, too.

1	C	oat flour
1	C	whole wheat flour
½	C	barley flour
½	C	rye flour
½	C	buckwheat flour
½	C	corn flour
¼	C	raw sunflower seeds
½	C	unsalted dry roasted peanuts
¼	C	raw cashew pieces
¼	C	chopped almonds
¼	C	chopped dried papaya
¼	C	chopped dried unsweetened pineapple
⅓	C	honey
¼	C	frozen unsweetened pineapple juice concentrate, thawed
¼	C	frozen unsweetened apple juice concentrate, thawed
½	C	water

1. Combine all ingredients; mix until smooth.

2. Roll into 1-tablespoon balls and wrap each in plastic wrap, or form in pancake-sized servings and store in plastic sandwich bags.

Yield: 110 individual snacks

	RCU	FU	Cal	%Fat	P	F	C	Na
Per Snack	0	0	27	30	1	1	4	T

3 Snacks = 1/2 Bread exchange; 1/2 Fat exchange

PEANUT BUTTER "CANDIES"

This is a tasty high-energy snack sure to be enjoyed by kids of all ages. Peanut butter "candies" can be enjoyed as a snack by children or those who are not trying to control their weight. (The peanut butter in the candies gives it a high fat content.)

¾	C	"natural" peanut butter
2	T	frozen unsweetened orange juice concentrate, thawed
6	T	frozen unsweetened apple juice concentrate, thawed
¾	tsp	vanilla
¾	C	instant nonfat dry milk
1	C	quick-cooking rolled oats
¼	C	sesame seeds
⅓	C	chopped walnuts or toasted almonds, optional

1. Blend peanut butter, orange juice concentrate, apple juice concentrate, and vanilla in a medium-size bowl. Add dry milk, oats, and sesame seeds; mix until thoroughly blended.

2. Roll mixture, about 1 tablespoon at a time, between palms of hands into small balls. Roll in chopped nuts. Place on waxed paper to dry. Place in paper candy cups. Refrigerate in a covered container.

Yield: 30 servings (1 ball per serving)

	RCU	FU	Cal	%Fat	P	F	C	Na
Per Serving	0	0	71	48.7	3	4	6	11

1 Serving = 1 Fat exchange

GENIEL'S SALSA

*This is a sweet, mild version of the famous salsas traditionally served in Mexican res-
taurants. Serve with homemade tortilla chips (see recipe) for a low-fat snack or appetizer.*

1. Peel and cut up 1/4 bushel tomatoes; cook down for about 1 hour.

2. Add 4 packages (1 box) dry Lipton tomato soup mix to cooked-down
    tomatoes. Cook together.

3. Grind in food processor:

4		green bell peppers
2	med	onions
3-4		hot chile peppers (hot green or jalapeno peppers); remove the seeds and wear rubber gloves to prevent skin irritation
2		garlic cloves
1		chili Tepeni, crushed (avoid skin contact)
½	C	cider vinegar
2	sm cans	diced Ortega chilies

4. Add ground mixture to tomatoes and cook until slightly thickened.

5. Freeze in freezer containers or bottle in jars and process.
    Process in water bath for about 35 minutes per pint.

Yield: 6 quarts or 48 (1/2-cup) servings

	RCU	FU	Cal	%Fat	P	F	C	Na
Per Serving	0	0	53	11	2	.6	12	91

1 Serving = 2 Vegetable exchange

OVEN-BAKED CORN CHIPS

Great and easy way to prepare fat-free and salt-free tortilla chips.

1 pkg corn tortillas

1. Cut each tortilla into 8 pie-shaped wedges.

2. Bake at 350° for 10 minutes.

3. Serve with Geniel's Salsa or a bean dip.

Yield: 12 servings (1 tortilla each)

	RCU	FU	Cal	%Fat	P	F	C	Na
Per Serving	0	0	67	15	2	1	13	53

1 Serving = 1 Bread exchange

CANNED PEACHES

As a sugar-free way to can fresh peaches, pour 1/4 cup frozen unsweetened apple juice concentrate, thawed, into each quart jar filled with prepared peaches. Fill the remainder of the jar with water. Process according to manufacturer's directions.

CANNED PEACHES II

For an alternative sugar-free method of canning fresh peaches, pour 1/4 cup frozen unsweetened pineapple juice concentrate, thawed, into each quart jar filled with prepared peaches. Fill the remainder of the jar with water. Process according to manufacturer's directions.

CHUNKY APPLESAUCE

This applesauce is delicious on toast, pancakes, waffles, in muffins, or eaten plain.

12	C	sliced apples, peeled and cored (it is best to use sweet apples, such as Golden Delicious, or a combination of Golden Delicious and Red Delicious or Rome Beauty)
¾	C	frozen unsweetened apple juice concentrate, thawed (use more if desired for a sweeter taste)
1	C	water cinnamon to taste

1. Place all ingredients in a heavy 6-quart pan.

2. Cook over low heat, stirring occasionally, until apple pieces are barely tender. Stir frequently to prevent scorching. Add more water if mixture seems too dry.

3. Extra applesauce may be bottled or frozen in plastic freezer bags.

Yield: 12 cups or 24 (1/2-cup) servings

	RCU	FU	Cal	%Fat	P	F	C	Na
Per Serving	0	0	46	4	T	T	12	2

1 Serving = 3/4 Fruit exchange

FRUITY POPCORN

This makes a tasty snack or a delicious gift!

1	T	margarine or butter, melted
½	tsp	cinnamon
7	C	popped corn, popped without salt or oil
1	6-oz pkg	Sun-Maid Fruit Bits (or 1 1/2 cups chopped dried mixed fruit)

1. Combine butter and cinnamon; stir well.

2. Drizzle over popped corn, tossing gently to coat.

3. Add chopped dried fruit and combine gently.

4. Store in an airtight container.

Yield: 8 (1-cup) servings

	RCU	FU	Cal	%Fat	P	F	C	Na
Per Cup	0	0	105	18	2	2	22	19

1 Cup = 1 Fruit exchange; 1/2 Bread exchange

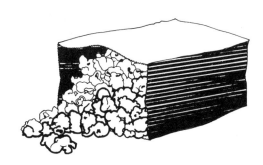

POPCORN SNACK

Great popcorn snack to be eaten with your favorite video.

8	C	popped corn (about 1/2 cup unpopped), popped without salt or oil
1½	C	bite-size crispy wheat squares (no sugar added)
1½	C	raisins
1	6-oz pkg	dried apricots, cut into fourths
¼	C	frozen unsweetened apple juice concentrate, thawed
2	T	margarine or butter, melted
1	tsp	cinnamon
¼	tsp	ginger

1. Combine 8 cups popped corn, wheat squares, raisins, and dried apricots in a large bowl; toss gently to combine.

2. Drizzle apple juice concentrate over popcorn mixture, tossing gently to coat.

3. Combine remaining ingredients; pour over popcorn mixture; toss gently to coat.

Yield: 12 (1-cup) servings

	RCU	FU	Cal	%Fat	P	F	C	Na
Per Cup	0	0	165	14	3	3	36	28

1 Cup = 1 1/2 Fruit exchange; 1/2 Bread exchange

NUTTY POPCORN

A snack for children or those not trying to control their weight. Nuts and peanut butter automatically make a recipe naturally higher in fats.

6	C	popped corn, popped without salt or oil
½	C	unsalted dry-roasted peanuts
½	C	toasty oat cereal
½	C	chopped dates
½	C	dried apples, chopped into small pieces
3	T	"natural" peanut butter
1	T	margarine or butter, melted

1. Combine popcorn, peanuts, oat cereal, dates, and apples; mix well.

2. Just before serving, combine peanut butter and margarine; heat in small saucepan until well combined. Drizzle peanut butter mixture over popcorn mixture; toss gently to coat.

Yield: 8 (1-cup) servings

	RCU	FU	Cal	%Fat	P	F	C	Na
Per Cup	0	1	184	46	5	9	22	38

1 Cup = 1/2 Fruit exchange; 1/2 Bread exchange; 1 1/2 Fat exchange

BLUEBERRY SOUP

A different type of appetizer with a great taste.

3	C	fresh or unsweetened frozen blueberries, thawed
1	8-oz can	unsweetened crushed pineapple, undrained
1	tsp	lemon juice
½	tsp	vanilla
2	T	frozen unsweetened apple juice concentrate, thawed
8	tsp	plain nonfat yogurt

1. Put 2 C of blueberries in blender container. Add pineapple, lemon juice, vanilla, and apple juice concentrate; blend until smooth.

2. Add the remaining 1 C of blueberries to the blender; mix well using a spoon or rubber spatula. Do not blend.

3. Pour the soup into chilled glass bowls and place 1 tsp nonfat yogurt on top of each serving.

4. Garnish with a sprig of fresh mint. Serve as an appetizer.

Yield: 8 (1/2-cup) servings

	RCU	FU	Cal	%Fat	P	F	C	Na
Per Serving	0	0	61	4	1	T	15	9

1 Serving = 1 Fruit exchange

CRANBERRY WALDORF

A festive fruit salad to accompany your Christmas holiday meals.

1½	C	chopped cranberries
1	C	chopped and cored red apple (do not peel)
1	C	chopped celery
1	C	halved seedless green grapes
¼	C	raisins
¼	C	coarsely chopped walnuts, optional
1	C	plain nonfat yogurt
¼	C	frozen unsweetened apple juice concentrate, thawed
¼	tsp	cinnamon

1. Combine first six ingredients.

2. Combine yogurt, juice concentrate, and cinnamon. Stir into the fruit mixture and toss gently to coat.

3. Cover and chill for 1 to 2 hours. Stir before serving.

Yield: 10 (1/2-cup) servings

	RCU	FU	Cal	%Fat	P	F	C	Na
Per Serving	0	0	62	3	2	T	15	31

1 Serving = 1 Fruit exchange

RICE FRUIT SALAD

Rice lovers will enjoy this salad.

3	C	cooked rice
1	15-oz can	unsweetened crushed pineapple
3	T	frozen unsweetened pineapple-orange-banana concentrate, thawed
2	T	cornstarch
½	tsp	vanilla
1	16-oz can	unsweetened fruit cocktail, drained
½	C	unsweetened coconut, optional
½	C	chopped walnuts, optional

1. Drain crushed pineapple, reserving juice; place reserved pineapple juice in saucepan (there should be about 1 cup). Add thawed juice concentrate; stir in cornstarch.

2. Bring to a boil, stirring constantly, until clear and thickened. Remove from heat and add vanilla. Cool.

3. Combine rice, drained pineapple, and fruit cocktail.

4. Just prior to serving, fold in cooled pineapple sauce. Add coconut and nuts if desired.

Yield: 10 servings

	RCU	FU	Cal	%Fat	P	F	C	Na
Per Serving	0	0	127	3	2	T	30	151

1 Serving = 1 Fruit exchange; 1 Bread exchange

Index

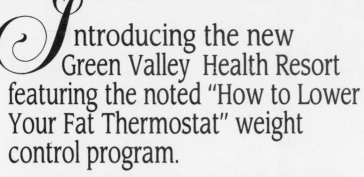
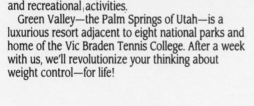

How To Lower Your Fat Thermostat

Diets don't work and you know it! The less you eat, the more your body clings to its fat stores. There is only one program that teaches you to eat to lose weight and it's detailed here in this nationwide best-selling book. All other weight-control programs are based on caloric deprivation. The *How To Lower Your Fat Thermostat* program is based on giving you enough total calories and nutrients to convince the control centers in your brain that regulate fat stores that you don't need to hold onto that fat any more. Then your weight will come down naturally and comfortably, and stay at that lower level permanently.

Recipes To Lower Your Fat Thermostat

Companion cookbook to *How To Lower Your Fat Thermostat*. Once you understand the principles of the fat thermostat program, you will want to put them to work in your daily diet. Now you can with this full-color, beautifully illustrated cookbook. New ways to prepare more than 400 of your favorite recipes. Breakfast ideas. Soups and salads. Meats and vegetables. Wok food, potatoes, beans, and breads. Desserts and treats. All designed to please and satisfy while lowering your fat thermostat.

Acrylic Cookbook Holder

This acrylic cookbook holder is the perfect companion to your new cookbook. Designed to hold any cookbook open without breaking the binding, it allows you to read recipes without distortion while protecting pages from splashes and spills.

Five Roadblocks to Weight Loss (Audiocassette)

If you have a serious weight problem that has failed to respond to the fat thermostat program, then you could be suffering from any of the five roadblocks to weight loss: food addictions, artificial sweeteners, food allergies, yeast overgrowth, and stress. Learn what these roadblocks are, what to do about them, and how the fat thermostat program relates to them . . . in an exclusive interview with Drs. Dennis Remington and Edward Parent.

Pocket Progress Guide

A pocket-sized summary of the fat thermostat program that includes food composition tables, daily records, and a progress summary for quick and easy reference and record-keeping anytime, anywhere.

The Neuropsychology of Weight Control
(8 Audiocassettes and Study Guide)

Based on the best-selling book, *How To Lower Your Fat Thermostat*, this audiocassette program explains the principles of the fat thermostat program, then teaches you how to reprogram your fat thermostat for leanness. You will learn how to take control of your body and mind, how to determine your ideal body image, how to develop a fat-burning mechanism in the brain, and—best of all—how to develop a lifelong blueprint for leanness and health.

The Neuropsychology of Weight Control
(Videocassette)

For some people, seeing is believing. While reviewing the key points of the program and the benefits of reaching your goal weight, this motivational video also features testimonials by people who have had dramatic success. In moments of doubt or discouragement, this video provides the needed support and encouragement.

The Bitter Truth About Artificial Sweeteners

Research proves that those people using artificial sweeteners tend to gain more weight. Not only do artificial sweeteners enhance the desire for sweets, they also cause many unpleasant side effects in addition to raising the fat thermostat. Learn the real truth about artificial sweeteners and sugars. Learn how they affect your health and weight and what you can do about them.

The Neuropsychology of Weight Control
Personal Progress Journal

The journal will be your year-long record of how well you're doing. It also provides information on nutrition, exercise and health.

Back To Health: A Comprehensive Medical and Nutritional Yeast-Control Program

If you suffer from anxiety, depression, memory loss, heartburn or gas . . . if you crave sugar, chocolate or alcohol . . . if weight control is a constant battle . . . if you are tired, weak and sore all over . . . this book was written for you. While yeast occurs naturally in the body, when out of control it becomes the body's enemy, manifesting itself in dozens of symptoms. Getting yeast back under control can correct many conditions once considered chronic. More than 100 yeast-free recipes, plus special sections on weight control, hypoglycemia and PMS.

SyberVision's Neuropsychology of Self-Discipline

The Master Key to Success

There's one critical characteristic that makes the difference between success and failure; self-discipline. Without it, you can never hope to achieve your ambitions. With it, there's no goal you can't reach. *The Neuropsychology of Self-Discipline* is a unique self-improvement program that allows you to instill a new and powerful self-mastery into your own mind and body. Armed with tools, insights, and skills of a highly disciplined achiever, you'll be able, for the first time in your life, to systematically pursue and successfully realize your most important goals.

Desserts to Lower Your Fat Thermostat

If you think you have to say goodbye to desserts, think again.

At last there's a book that lets you have your cake and eat it too. *Desserts to Lower Your Fat Thermostat* is filled with what you thought you could never find: recipes for delicious desserts, snacks, and treats that are low in fat and free of sugar, salt, and artificial sweeteners.

The two hundred delectable ideas packed between the covers of this book meet the guidelines of both the American Heart Association and the American Diabetes Association. They will meet your own tough standards too — especially if you've been longing for winning ideas that will delight your family without destroying their health.

Gifford's Gourmet De-Lites

Vitality House is pleased to offer you an exciting work from a professional chef, Howard Gifford, whose meals have astonished guests lowering their fat thermostats at the Green Valley Health Resort. Says Howard, "I love to create that which is pleasing both to the eye and the palate. Preparing healthy food is my medium! My tools? The common everyday household kitchen conveniences found in most American homes today. 'Simplicity' is my watchword.

Become the creative gourmet cook you have always wanted to be! Learn what the magic of using just the right spices, extracts and natural juices can do for your foods! I'll also give you some helpful hints for shopping and organizing."

Qty.	Code	Description	Retail	Subtotal
	A	How To Lower Your Fat Thermostat	$9.95	
	B	Recipes To Lower Your Fat Thermostat	$14.95	
	C	Acrylic Cookbook Holder	$9.95	
	D	Neuropsychology of Weight Control (8 Audiocassettes and Study Guide) ✱	$69.95	
	E	Back To Health	$9.95	
	G	Bitter Truth About Artificial Sweeteners	$9.95	
	H	Five Roadblocks to Weight Loss (Audiocassette)	$7.95	
	I	Pocket Progress Guide	$2.95	
	J	Neuropsychology of Weight Control (Videocassette)	$29.95	
	L	Neuropsychology of Self-Discipline ✱	$69.95	
	M	Personal Progress Journal	$14.95	
	N	Desserts to Lower Your Fat Thermostat	$12.95	
	O	Gifford's Gourmet De-Lites	$12.95	
	Z	Green Valley Health Resort Information Packet	FREE	
		Shipping and handling, $2.00 for the first item. (Within the United States)		$2.00
		Add an additional $.50 per item thereafter.		+
		Utah residents add 6.25% sales tax.		+
Prices subject to change without notice.			TOTAL	

✱Purchase code "D" or code "L" and obtain your choice of a FREE book up to $14.95 in value. Be sure to indicate which book you would like!

☐ Check ☐ Money Order ☐ MasterCard ☐ VISA ☐ American Express

Card No. _____ Expires _____

Signature _____ Phone _____

Ship to: Name _____

Address _____

City/State/Zip _____

Mail to: Vitality House International, 1675 North Freedom Blvd. #11-C Provo, Utah 84604 (801) 373-5100

To Order: Call Toll Free 1-800-637-0708.